Banning Liebscher is a leader I want to follow. He's a vision caster. A man who knows Jesus and is so hungry for others to know him in the same way. This book answers the questions our entire generation has been wrestling with. "What does it look like to live our best life?" and "What does it look like to courageously align ourselves with holiness and faith?" This book will cast a vision for your life that will alter everything. I'm thankful for leaders like Banning who lead the way.

—MACK BROCK, worship leader

Banning challenges the prevailing lie that happiness is found in wealth and pleasure. He points us in the right direction that abundant life is found as we fully engage with Christ.

—LISA BEVERE, *New York Times* bestselling author

I use the phrase "living my best life" a lot! So when Banning, a man I have come to respect and admire, speaks about how to truly do so, I know to listen. Through my battles with depression, he has become someone who shines his bright light into the dark places in my soul. He has done it once again with his timely, relatable, deep, yet practical book. Read it and go on an incredible journey to your best life.

—MANDISA, national recording artist and speaker

After a ten-year hiatus from the recording industry, I've been searching for reasons to reengage, reasons to once again answer the call to this vein of ministry in my life. Based on what I'd seen and experienced, I lacked courage. I allowed fear and the lies of the enemy to derail my relentless pursuit to answer the call.

What the Holy Spirit so graciously conveys through Banning in this book has catapulted me into a place of obedience and willingness to answer the call once again. I am bold, strong, and God is with me. The joy I find in the journey is the realization of his grace and the fact that I'm chosen not because of my merit or goodness but because I simply decided to answer.

I'm called to serve the local church by training and developing creatives therein. This book affirmed me on my three-mile walk toward it all.

—DARWIN HOBBS, worship pastor and recording artist

This book should be in everyone's hands. Inside each of us is a longing to live a fulfilling life, and yet we don't always know how to live it out. In this book, Banning lays out a clear path of how we as followers of Jesus can live in this day and age, and live our best life in a way that defies human reasoning. I'm so grateful this book is now in your hands.

—ERIC JOHNSON, Bethel Church

This book isn't for observers. It's a call to the ones ready to count the cost. Knowing Banning for more than twenty years, I can attest that he has lived every word in this book himself. Not swayed by crowds or numbers, he has dedicated his life to the gospel of Jesus Christ. This book maps the journey we must take if we really want to take the three-mile walk. Banning is undoubtedly the kind of spiritual father our generation has been crying out for. He illuminates the good without hiding the hard stuff, equipping us for both risk and triumph. I am confident this book is a resource that will be in your library for years to come.

—HAVILAH CUNNINGTON, founder, Truth to Table

Banning is a brilliant communicator and has again proven that he has an incredible gift in articulating the profound truths written in this book, truths that will help you discover the call of God on your life and help you take the right steps to seeing your destiny realized. Taking the narrow road is often looked at as hard and irrelevant in today's culture, but it is the path that leads to a blessed and fulfilled life. This book is a must-read for this generation.

—ALEX SEELEY, author; lead pastor,
The Belonging Co. Church, Nashville

—

THE THREE-MILE WALK

—

BANNING LIEBSCHER

THE THREE-MILE WALK

THE COURAGE YOU NEED TO LIVE
THE LIFE GOD WANTS FOR YOU

ZONDERVAN
BOOKS

ZONDERVAN BOOKS

The Three-Mile Walk
Copyright © 2020 by Banning Liebscher

Requests for information should be addressed to:
Zondervan, 3900 Sparks Dr. SE, Grand Rapids, Michigan 49546

Zondervan titles may be purchased in bulk for educational, business, fundraising, or sales promotional use. For information, please email SpecialMarkets@Zondervan.com.

ISBN 978-0-310-35850-3 (audio)

Library of Congress Cataloging-in-Publication Data

Names: Liebscher, Banning, author.
Title: The three-mile walk : the courage you need to live the life God wants for you / Banning Liebscher.
Description: Grand Rapids : Zondervan, 2020. | Includes bibliographical references. | Summary: "We are all called to change the world, yet many of us don't know how to begin. Jesus Culture founder and pastor Banning Liebscher reveals the three moves that will propel you into the adventure of a lifetime with a heart fully alive, a life fully engaged, and the courage needed for both"-- Provided by publisher.
Identifiers: LCCN 2020001825 (print) | LCCN 2020001826 (ebook) | ISBN 9780310358480 (hardcover) | ISBN 9780310358497 (ebook)
Subjects: LCSH: Christian life.
Classification: LCC BV4501.3 .L54145 2020 (print) | LCC BV4501.3 (ebook) | DDC 248.4--dc23
LC record available at https://lccn.loc.gov/2020001825
LC ebook record available at https://lccn.loc.gov/2020001826

Published in association with the literary agency of The Fedd Agency, Post Office Box 341973, Austin, TX 78734.

Cover design: Jeff Miller | Faceout Studio
Cover photos: Kryshtofor Volodymyr | Wilqkuku | Shutterstock | Unsplash
Interior design: Denise Froehlich

Printed in the United States of America

20 21 22 23 24 25 26 27 28 29 30 /LSC/ 15 14 13 12 11 10 9 8 7 6 5 4 3 2 1

I dedicate this book to the inaugural class of the Jesus Culture School of Leadership.

Your passion to engage your calling with holiness, courage, and faith is inspiring.

May you continue to take the three-mile walk with Jesus and do all He has put in your hearts.

Contents

Acknowledgments

Jesus Culture Sacramento: This message was birthed from all we have been pursuing as a church community. It's an honor to be able to export it to others.

SeaJay, Ellianna, Raya, Lake, and the Jesus Culture staff: You are those most directly affected by the reality that producing a book requires me to disappear for months on end. I'm so grateful for the strength and grace you carry that keeps our world turning. Thank you.

Allison Armerding, my editor: I couldn't do this without you. You carry my heart and message brilliantly and make me look way better than I am. Thank you for coming alongside me and my desire to strengthen and encourage the church to see revival in our day.

Becky Johnson and Phil Manginelli: You helped me shape this message. Thank you for letting me throw my ideas off you and giving me excellent input.

Esther Fedorkevich, Whitney Gossett, and the team at Zondervan: Thank you for making this book possible.

Introduction

I think it was Oprah who first popularized the phrase "Live your best life." Social media overflows with posts of people announcing, "Living my best life!"—typically with photos of them eating amazing food, taking exotic vacations, or going to epic concerts, games, or shows. Others show them achieving their goals for self-improvement and self-actualization—getting fit at the gym, earning a degree, getting married, or starting a business.

This is pretty much the vision of the good life or best life in our wealthy, secular, individualistic culture. We are chasing happiness in exciting and pleasurable experiences, and we're chasing purpose and fulfillment in achieving success.

However, despite what we show or see on the social media highlight reels, none of the things we're chasing are leading us to a life that is vibrant, thriving, fulfilling, and truly the best. Instead more and more of us are battling anxiety and depression. We're feeding addictions to our electronic devices, distracting ourselves from our struggle to live without a sense of deep purpose and meaning. Psychologists and social scientists are telling us that we're wired for belonging and connection, but these experiences seem more and more elusive in our selfish, disconnected, transient, stressed-out, busy lifestyles.

It couldn't be more obvious that our culture's vision of the best life has some major flaws. However, people won't break out of the hopeless cycle of chasing happiness and meaning in temporary stuff and success unless they see a better option. This is where the people of God are called to shine. We have access to the truth that living our best life is found first in pursuing God above all else and surrendering to His plan for our lives. In God's kingdom, the way to self-actualization is not the way of achieving success but the way of discovering who the Father says we are as His sons and daughters and living out of that identity and relationship with Him. Likewise, the way to joy and happiness is not the way of collecting pleasurable experiences but the way of laying our lives down in sacrificial love.

However, many believers are not living deeply into the truth of who they are called to be and what they are called to do in the kingdom of God, at least not deeply enough that they begin to experience and bear the fruit of the abundant life, the best life, Jesus promised us. In so many cases, when the world looks at us, they see the same anxiety, depression, struggle, striving, insecurity, busyness, and distraction they are living under. When the church starts to look like the world—when, in Jesus' words, we lose our saltiness and become lukewarm—it is because we have ceased to be fully engaged in the call of God on our lives.

I don't think our lack of full engagement is just a clarity problem. Jesus' call to every believer is simple enough to understand. He calls us to follow Him, walk with Him, obey Him, and imitate Him in thought, word, and deed. Confusion and compromise set in not because we fail to understand the call but because the call is challenging to live out. It requires a conversion of the heart that produces a transformed life, a conversion that takes place not in a moment but over a lifetime of walking with Jesus. A converted, whole, healthy heart, not a head full of biblical knowledge, is what motivates us to be fully engaged in our call.

In this book, we're going to look at three aspects of this converted heart. Each aspect is a word you're probably familiar with. Again, for most of us the challenge lies not in understanding the definitions of these spiritual words (though in some areas clarification and correction is needed, and we'll cover that too) but in living them out. First, a fully engaged heart is completely set apart for God; it is *holy*. Second, a fully engaged heart will risk and endure pain and difficulty; it is *courageous*. And third, a fully engaged heart is anchored in unseen reality and trusts it over and above seen reality; it is full of *faith*. Holiness, courage, and faith—these are the three "miles" of the heart journey we must walk to fulfill our call.

My heart burns with passion to see a generation fully engaged in their call, not just because it's what we're supposed to be doing as Christians but because that's where we thrive. I know from experience that once you experience the fully engaged life of walking with Jesus into all that He has for you, you are ruined for anything less. Let's head out on this three-mile walk together!

1

—

The First Step

There are moments that mark us, change the trajectory of our lives, and ultimately define us. Sometimes these moments crash in on us, loud and obvious. Sometimes they begin subtly and slowly crescendo. Sometimes they come in answer to our prayers and cries, and other times they blindside us when we least expect it. But however and whenever these moments come, we cannot deny that afterward something is different inside us. Our hearts have been awakened to the call of God on our life.

As I look back on my life, I see marking moments when God awakened something inside me. The first happened when I was seventeen. Someone gave me a biography of Billy Graham, and I wept through the whole book; I couldn't put it down. The same thing happened when I read the biography of Dr. Martin Luther King Jr. I found myself lying on the ground, weeping, wrecked by his courage and self-sacrifice. Throughout my late teens and early twenties, there were many occasions when I ended up weeping: when I read books like Frank Bartleman's book on revival and Kathryn Kuhlman's biography, when I heard preachers like Mike Bickle speak on holiness and Lou Engle teach on intercession for revival, and when leader after leader called me out in meetings and spoke words over me, describing what they were seeing and sensing about God's call for my life. In every case, my heart wasn't simply being moved; it was being marked by a passionate hunger. I didn't have all the words to describe what was happening to me in these experiences; I just knew something had awakened inside me. Later I recognized that these were moments when God was calling me, speaking to me, and waking up my heart to His purpose for my life. My heart was saying, *I too want to change the world. I want to be a leader whose life makes a difference. I want to give myself to prayer for an entire generation to be awakened by the love and power of God. I want what these people have lived and are talking about.*

If you are a follower of Jesus, you have probably experienced moments like these, even if you didn't recognize them—moments when your heart was moved with desire. You have sensed that voice inside you saying, *This is it. This is what you were made for.* You have heard the call of God on your life. If you haven't, then my prayer is that while reading this book, you will experience a marking moment that stirs your heart and ignites courage to follow Jesus with all of your heart. If you have had that moment, then my prayer is this: I want you to fully engage the call of God on your life. We are at our best when we are fully engaged in becoming who God has called us to become and doing what God has called us to do.

It's easy to assume that when you've been awakened to your call, you'll engage your call. That is the logical progression. However, not everyone fully engages their call throughout their lives. Many stall out, give up, or never really say yes to the journey of experiencing all that God has for them. I wrote this book because I am passionate about helping you avoid the pitfalls that keep you from full engagement. I want you to be fully engaged in your call not just for a moment but for a lifetime.

Jonathan and His Armor-Bearer

One of my favorite Bible stories that paints a picture of what it looks like to fully engage the call of God on our lives is the story of Jonathan and his armor-bearer, told in 1 Samuel 14.

When this story begins, King Saul has led Israel to war with the Philistines, the old enemy God called the Israelites to drive out of the promised land. After an initial successful attack on a Philistine outpost, things have not gone well. The Israelite army is outnumbered six hundred to "six thousand charioteers, and soldiers as numerous as the sand on the seashore" (1 Sam. 13:5). Saul has been demoralized after disobeying God and making sacrifices before the prophet Samuel could arrive and is just sitting under a pomegranate tree, seemingly without a plan of action. The Philistine army is fully equipped with weapons, while Saul and Jonathan are the only men in the Israelite army with swords and spears. Now the two armies are encamped on the opposite ends of a treacherous three-mile pass, and fear is building in the Israelite camp as they sit, waiting for the upcoming battle.

It's in this moment that something stirs in the heart of Jonathan, and he decides to take action. "Then Jonathan said to the young man who bore his armor, 'Come, let us go over to the garrison of these uncircumcised; it may be that the LORD will work for us. For nothing restrains the LORD from saving by many or by few.' So his armorbearer said to him, 'Do all that is in your heart. Go then; here I am with you, according to your heart'" (1 Sam. 14:6–7 NKJV).

Jonathan has an awakening moment. He's looking at the circumstances—the terrified Israelite soldiers, his defeated father unwilling or unable to lead the charge, and the superior army about to crush them—yet he is not intimidated and overwhelmed with despair. Instead something inside him is provoked. A conviction awakens that says, *Even though the odds are against us, I refuse to passively look from a distance at what I have been called to do. I am the son of the king, leader of the armies of Israel. I am called to fight and defeat the enemies of God's people. Nothing about these circumstances changes that call; in fact, now is exactly the time to engage it.*

Jonathan is no longer content to remain on the sideline of his destiny. He has to get up and do something about it. He invites one faithful companion, his armor-bearer, on a special ops surgical strike against the Philistine outpost. Together the two friends pick their way across the rocky, dangerous three-mile pass (if you want a visual, look up the Michmash pass on the internet; it looks a lot like the canyon where Indiana Jones was chasing the bad guys in *Raiders of the Lost Ark*). Then Jonathan suggests that they engage the army with a risky but divinely inspired strategy: they'll stand at the bottom of the cliff below the outpost, in full sight of their enemies, agreeing that if the Philistines call them to climb up to their camp, they'll take it as a sign that God is giving them the victory. "So both of them showed themselves to the Philistine outpost. 'Look!' said the Philistines. 'The Hebrews are crawling out of the holes they were hiding in.' The men of the outpost shouted to Jonathan and his armor-bearer, 'Come up to us and we'll teach you a lesson.' So Jonathan said to his armor-bearer, 'Climb up after me; the LORD has given them into the hand of Israel'" (1 Sam. 14:11–12).

Jonathan and his armor-bearer don't even try to be stealthy or protect themselves as they climb the steep cliff with their hands and feet. When they reach the top, Jonathan rushes into the battle with his armor-bearer right behind him, both killing man after man. In no time, twenty dead Philistines lie scattered on the ground.

The battle doesn't end there, however; it's just begun. It's at this point where God intervenes and shows up directly in the fight. He sends the Philistines into a panic, and they start to slaughter each other. Soon word of their sudden, bizarre self-destruction reaches King Saul, and he finally decides to get up from under the pomegranate tree and lead his men to the battle. As the day progresses, more and more men join the Israelite army. Some are traitors who defected to the Philistines and decide to return to Saul and Jonathan after watching the enemy destroy themselves. Others are scared Israelites who have been hiding in the hills and, upon hearing that the Philistines are on the run, gain the courage to join the Israelites pursuing them (1 Sam. 14:17–23). In the end Israel wins the day and the whole tide of the war turns, all because one man decided to step out of the safety of the camp and engage the call on his life.

Jonathan's story is a story for all of us. He is an example of how to engage the call of God on our lives and what's at stake for us in engaging that call. As we journey together through this book, we'll be looking closer at each step of the journey Jonathan took that day with his armor-bearer, and what it means for us in our journey. To understand what Jonathan did, however, we first need to understand his mindset and motivations. What caused Jonathan to no longer be satisfied sitting idly by and stirred him to begin that three-mile walk?

I see four key internal postures, or attitudes, that shaped the way Jonathan engaged his call. He *took ownership* of his call, he *dreamed* of his call, he *counted the cost* of his call, and he *was provoked* by his call. These four movements are critical if we are to engage the call of God on our lives.

Step 1: Own the Call

Let me be crystal clear. If you are a believer in Jesus, you have a call of God on your life. This call has two dimensions—identity and mission. You are first called to *be* somebody—to fully identify as a son or daughter of the Father, just like Jesus. Operating from that relational identity in turn defines what you are called to *do*—your mission, which is connected to the corporate mission of the people of God. Every member of God's family is called to partner with Him to impact the world with the reality of His kingdom. He has destined you to do great things with Him, to do the impossible, and to overcome evil with good. He has called you to change the world.

You will never fulfill your call to be and to do simply by knowing about your call, however. You must take ownership of your identity and mission. Ownership is a mindset that generates an attitude of authority, initiative, and responsibility. Someone who owns their call thinks, *Nobody else can be a son or daughter for me. Nobody else can fulfill my mission to change the world. That's my job.* Owners do not sit around waiting for someone else to live their Christian life for them. They have been given resources, opportunities, and responsibilities to accomplish what God has called them to.

One of the things I, as a pastor and leader in the body of Christ, have a passion for is to see believers cultivate an ownership mindset. We will never see the harvest God desires or impact cities at the level we should without every believer taking ownership of their call. It is the job of the saints to do the work of ministry, and the job of spiritual leaders to equip and encourage them to do this job (Eph. 4:11–12). Unfortunately, I typically find this ownership mindset lacking in church culture. Instead many Christians are being trained to think that it's spiritual leaders' responsibility to fulfill the identity and mission God has given them.

When we planted Jesus Culture Sacramento, personal responsibility was one of our founding core values. In those early days, we out of necessity kept things simple (and still do)—Sunday services, children's ministry, and some larger community gatherings.

We didn't immediately build a small group structure or implement the normal church programs. We knew that as the church grew, we would add more structure and communities to serve people. Our goal was to make sure any structure we were building was equipping people to do the work of the ministry rather than doing the ministry for them. The vision was to build people, not just programs, and see what our people produced.

It was fascinating to see the response of people who had been in church for years. Not everyone who came at the beginning was unchurched or unsaved. Many of them knew how church works. It was not uncommon for people to approach me, asking how they could get plugged into community. Since we didn't have a small group structure built at that time and things were fairly basic, I encouraged them to invite someone out to coffee or over for dinner. Many of them just looked at me in confusion; they were expecting me to tell them about the systems and structures we had in place for them to find community and weren't sure what to do when we didn't have that. Others came to me, asking where our new believers' class was; they had a neighbor or coworker who had recently received Christ and were looking for the class they should send them to so they could be discipled. Since we didn't have a new believers' class, my response was something like, "The new believers' class is in your living room, and you're leading it." I had other people ask what our church was doing for the poor. I assured them that we believe deeply in our mandate as the body of Christ to care for the poor. But when I started telling them stories of what individual people in the congregation were doing to serve the church in our city, they seemed unimpressed. What they had really wanted to know was, "What is the corporation of the church doing for the poor? What programs do you run for the poor?"

Hear me: I am not opposed to small groups, new believers'

classes, or programs to care for the poor. This is not a commentary on that. Many churches run incredible programs to connect people and serve their city that are having tremendous impact. I'm also not opposed to systems and structure; we have both at our church. What I am opposed to is systems and structure that communicate it's someone else's responsibility to do what God has called you to do. With good intentions, we build structures in the church that are not equipping people to live out the call on their lives but rather are stepping in to fulfill that call. As a result, people begin to think that what God has called them to do is someone else's responsibility.

When you got saved, you became a follower and disciple of Jesus, which means He is the one you are to learn from and imitate. Every follower of Jesus is called to pray, gather in community, share their faith, disciple others, pray for the sick, take care of the poor, further the ministry of reconciliation, and be generous and faithful with their finances. This may be news to you, but it's not the pastor's job to disciple your neighbor. That's part of the call on your life. But we have a generation of people who have grown up thinking that it's the church's job to live out their Christian life for them. If your church never had a small group structure, would you still gather with other believers simply because that's what Jesus asks? If your church didn't have a program to take care of the poor, would you ask God what you are to do for the poor in your city because that's your call as a follower of Jesus? Your answers are probably a good indicator of the degree to which you've been encouraged to develop an ownership mentality.

I want to challenge you. When you see an area of lack in the church and think, *The church should be doing something about this*, stop yourself before you go to someone and start complaining about it. Instead take it to the Lord and ask Him, "God, are You highlighting this area of need to me because You want me to do something about it?" Then do whatever He says. Maybe He just wants you to pray that the need will be met. Maybe He wants to show you others who are already working on the problem so you can partner with them. Or maybe He wants you to pioneer something new and build a solution. Whatever it is, you can be sure that it will look like you stepping up and taking ownership and responsibility, not standing on the sideline, critiquing and complaining.

God has called you to be someone, and He has called you to do something. But that call will never fully manifest unless you take ownership of it. One of the signs that we truly have been awakened to our call is that we have a growing sense of ownership of what God has called us to. The idea of sitting back and waiting for others to take the initiative before we act becomes less and less satisfying to us. Like Jonathan, we see that engaging our call is our responsibility.

Note: Taking ownership of the call doesn't mean that we go alone! Jonathan didn't set out to face the Philistines by himself. He didn't need an army, but he knew he needed at least one other guy to partner with him in his mission. As we engage in our call to be and do what God has called us to be and do, relationships will always be a critical part of that journey. We need people around us who have our backs, like Jonathan's armor-bearer, and we need to have their backs too. We can't start putting the ownership and responsibility for our part of those relationships on others.

Step 2: Dream of the Call

Jonathan didn't just have a sense of responsibility to act; he had a desire to act. His call was connected to the dreams of his heart. His armor-bearer recognized this and encouraged him, "Do all that is in your heart" (1 Sam. 14:7 NKJV).

You will never be satisfied until you are engaging the call of God on your life, because your call is connected to the dreams He has placed in your heart. This is what is happening in those awakening moments: your innermost dreams and desires are waking up and stirring your emotions and imagination to start envisioning and pursuing what He's put inside you. It's a heart awakening, not an intellectual awakening.

Years ago the Lord began to tell me that He was releasing dreamers again in the body of Christ. I began to wonder what a dreamer looked like. So of course I thought of children. Children are natural dreamers. I have three kids myself. When you have children, you begin to realize very quickly that they love to dream, and to dream big. If I asked one of my daughters when she was little, "What do you want to be when you grow up?" she responded with the most audacious things, like, "I want to be an astronaut and walk on the moon!" All my kids had big dreams.

When we are children, dreaming seems to come naturally; however, something happens when we transition to adulthood that causes many of us to lose our ability to dream. The way I put it is that we get introduced to "reality." When my daughter came to me and told me she wanted to be an astronaut, I patted her on the head and said, "Sweetie, you can be whatever you put your mind to." I didn't want to crush her dreams. But I didn't really believe my daughter would achieve that dream, because as an adult, I knew something she didn't know. I knew the odds of her becoming an astronaut. I knew the stories of people who tried to be astronauts and failed. So even though I didn't say it out loud, I thought, *Sweetie, there are 320 million people in this nation, and only a handful become astronauts. Unfortunately, you have even less of a chance if you're a female. Let's be more realistic and find something else to do.* My ability to dream with her was greatly hindered because of this thing called reality.

But Jonathan wasn't confined to the realm of odds and statistics. This doesn't mean he was in denial about his chances of success in taking on the Philistine army with one other guy. He simply knew there was Someone with them who was not confined to the human definition of reality. On their own, Jonathan and his armor-bearer couldn't save Israel, but Jonathan knew that God can save "whether by many or by few" (1 Sam. 14:6). Jonathan was connected to the truth that God is not confined to the realm of odds and statistics. I can imagine that as Jonathan made the three-mile walk across that valley, he wrestled with reality the way we all do when we start to pursue the dreams in our hearts. Yet he continued to trust that the dream God had put in his heart was possible, because the God of the impossible was with him. We must do the same.

Seeing a church that is not afraid to dream has been a passion of mine since I began ministry. Years ago I had a nighttime dream in which I saw people with wells of dreams inside them, but they were capped by lids. As I was preaching, I was reaching inside people and pulling the caps off the wells of their dreams. I believe God is uncapping His people's ability to dream by encountering them with His greater reality—the reality that sets them free from the limits of human reality. For too long, they've lived under the delusion that God is somehow bound by these limits. They think He's intimidated by the obstacles facing them or by their own weaknesses, that He can't redeem the years of sin, poverty, addiction, oppression, or other issues that have clung to their family line. But God is breaking that lie and unlocking a childlike belief that sees the truth: they are called to overcome these impossibilities with Him. As the dreams of their hearts awaken, they will begin to look at impossible situations and say, "God can save by many or by few. Nothing is impossible with Him." This belief will set them free to step out on the three-mile walk, knowing they are not alone.

Something we must settle in our hearts is that the call of God on our lives was designed to be fulfilled through partnership with Him, which means that if we try to imagine fulfilling it on our own, it will seem impossible. The call of God on your life *is* impossible without God! The person He is calling you to be is impossible apart from Him, and the thing He is calling you to do is impossible apart from Him. But the good news is that you are not apart from Him. This is the reality you must encounter that will uncap your ability to dream of doing the impossible with Him.

Encountering the real presence of God and hearing His voice is the center of the Christian life. One of the greatest tragedies in Christianity is that the gospel often gets reduced to a transactional relationship instead of an intimate relationship. God gives us forgiveness of sin and entrance to heaven, and in exchange we serve Him, which usually means doing a laundry list of spiritual activities like going to church, reading our Bibles, giving to the needy, being kind to our neighbors. This falls so far short of what Jesus died to give us—a real, dynamic, ever-growing, transformational, heart-to-heart connection with God in which we walk with Him, hear Him speak to our hearts, encounter His presence and love in tangible ways, and learn to make our home in Him (John 15:4). Building, strengthening, and living from this connection is the purpose behind every spiritual discipline we practice. If your Bible study, prayer time, church and Bible study attendance, fasting, and other spiritual activities are not leading you into real encounters with the presence and voice of God in which He awakens, speaks to, and transforms your heart, then you need to adjust something. These should be providing you with what you need in order to see and engage your call with an awakened heart and the awareness that the God of the impossible is with you, leading you and empowering you.

Your heart has the ability to trust God and His reality beyond what your mind can comprehend. If you've ever really been around somebody who is a dreamer, somebody who is engaging the call of God on their life, it's quite likely that they have appeared to be out of their mind. It's because they are engaging the things in their heart, not just in their mind. I'm not suggesting that we stop thinking or that we don't intelligently look at things. But our minds need to defer to what God is awakening in our hearts. Jonathan's armor-bearer understood this. This is why he did not tell him, "Do all that's in your mind. Do all that makes sense. Do only what's safe." He said, "Do all that is in your heart." If I had been walking with Jonathan in that moment, I probably would have said, "Jonathan, what are you thinking? There's an entire army of the Philistines, and it's you with one other guy. This doesn't make sense at all. You're out of your mind." But dreamers understand that even though it may sound crazy from a rational standpoint, from the heart it makes complete sense.

You may have a dream to write books that will impact the lives of thousands. People may look at you and say, "You didn't even do well in English at school. Are you out of your mind?" But your heart knows that this is the call on your life. You may have a desire to be a good father or a good mother, but your family heritage is one of brokenness and abuse. You may have a dream in your heart to start a business or a nonprofit, and people may look at you and say, "You have no money." It may not make sense, but it's the dream God has placed in your heart. It's time for you to believe that He is with you to do all according to your heart.

Pay attention to what's in your heart. Whatever stirs and moves you is connected to your dreams. A mentor of mine once said, "Pay attention to your tears, because they are the windows into your soul." Any strong emotion can move us to tears—longing, excitement, sorrow, or even anger. I pay attention to what moves me and listen to hear if God is speaking to me through that. I don't dismiss the things that stir me—a preacher who says something that fills me with hope, a news story about injustice that burdens me to pray, a movie scene that breaks my heart, or books that awaken my imagination and passion. Instead of allowing these moments to pass me by, I ask myself why I am responding to them this way. Many times, I find that there is something in them connected to the dreams of my heart and the call on my life.

What opportunities move you with desire? What problems and injustices in the world ignite your anger? What stories break your heart? God might be speaking to you about the issue of orphans and foster care. Then, without any planning, you happen to watch two movies in a row in which foster care is an integral part of the storyline. Or the topic just happens to come up in conversations with people. Every time foster care shows up, you find your heart stirred with a deep emotion. God is trying to awaken something inside you. Pay attention to that, and ask Him to show you how He's inviting you to dream about the call on your life.

Step 3: Count the Cost of the Call

Have you ever stepped out to pursue a dream and experienced initial success, only to have things turn scary in a hurry? That's what happened to Jonathan. First Samuel 13:3 tells us that it was Jonathan who had led the first attack on the Philistines in this particular war. Saul had jumped on his success and announced it with trumpets throughout the land, which apparently was like waving a red flag at a bull. The Philistines wasted no time in amassing their superior army and declaring war, frightening Saul and the Israelites out of their minds. It looked like shedding first blood was going to backfire on Saul and Jonathan big-time. As Jonathan considered going up for this second attack with his armor-bearer, he had to count the cost. Would he be risking his life again, only to see their situation get even worse? In the end he said, "Yes. It's worth it."

Early in my journey with Jesus Culture, God put a dream in my heart that we would see stadiums filled with a generation seeking God. We had, and still have, a passion to see people mobilized to encounter God and be equipped for revival. After years of doing conferences in our hometown and around the world, in 2011 we stepped out and held our first gathering in an arena—a three-day conference at Allstate Arena in Chicago. A gathering of that size and scope requires a lot of planning, which required a commitment from us two years in advance. When I said yes to Chicago in 2009, I really didn't know what I was saying yes to. I was excited about the possibility of thousands gathering in an arena, and I was pursuing a dream God had awakened in my heart, but I didn't understand what pursuing that dream would cost. Up to that point, our conferences had been held in churches or midsize theater venues. The most we had gathered was a little more than two thousand people. Now we were going to gather in an arena that could hold fifteen thousand people and spend ten times anything we had ever spent on an event. I remember walking into the empty arena the day before the conference and being struck by the weight of what my yes two years earlier meant. I realized while I looked around that arena that this could have gone a different direction. People could have not come. Finances could have not been there. I knew we had taken a risk, but I didn't know how big that risk was when we committed to it. And in the end, it paid off. We ended up having fourteen thousand people attend. Even though it was the most pressure I had ever experienced in ministry up to that point, it was a beautiful and powerful event, a marking moment in my life and in the lives of many others. I still run into people who tell me how God encountered them and awakened things in their hearts through the worship and messages preached at that one gathering, and they have never been the same.

But the story didn't end there. Right after our conference ended in Chicago, God spoke to my heart to gather again the following year, this time in two locations. And we did. We gathered outside New York City in an arena that held thirteen thousand and in Los Angeles at a large theater venue. This time we had a different outcome. I don't view those two gatherings as failures, because we were obedient, stepped out in faith, and did what God had asked of us, and many people's lives were changed. But this time the venues weren't full and the finances weren't there. The year leading up to those two gatherings, our team was under tremendous pressure, and it showed. It felt like bolts were popping out of our structure both relationally and organizationally. I had to navigate the embarrassment of having venues that were not full, and I experienced an unprecedented level of anxiety around finances. All of these things made me feel the cost of my yes more acutely.

Paying the price to pursue our dreams and engage the call on our life can be uncomfortable, exhausting, scary, and—yes—painful. When we experience this pain, the danger is that we'll stop dreaming and taking risks. The aftermath of our New York and Los Angeles gatherings brought me to a point of decision. Would I keep saying yes to the dreams God had put in my heart, now that I knew just how much it could cost not only me but our entire team? Or would I shut down those dreams to play it safe? I knew what the decision had to be. God still required me to move forward and engage His call on my life. So I told Him and our team, "I'm going to keep dreaming and keep saying yes. I don't want to shrink back because I stepped out once and it didn't work out like I thought." Since that point, I know better what I am saying yes to when I step out to pursue a dream in obedience to His call. But being aware of the cost only makes my obedience a greater gift I now offer to God.

We must discover that the call of God on our life is worth the price of failure and disappointment. We will face both on this three-mile walk. Things will not work out as we planned and will probably leave us feeling discouraged or disillusioned. But we can't allow those experiences to kill our hope and convince us to pull back. If we allow disappointment to shape our future decisions, we will no longer dream, because it is too risky. We must be prepared to endure disappointment and continue the walk.

I remember a disappointing experience I had years ago, when my firstborn was still a small baby. It's a silly story but one that illustrates what it looks like to be excited and passionate about a dream and experience disappointment. We were vacationing with some friends on the coast of Oregon when I saw an advertisement for a whale watching excursion. It was an hour-long boat ride in the bay, during which we would be able to see a whale up close. That sounded exciting, so we bought the tickets. After we climbed on board with our baby girl, however, I made a big mistake. I took our baby down into the cabin to hold her as the boat took off. Within five minutes I was horribly seasick and on the verge of throwing up.

I went back up on the deck and did all I could to hold it together. Soon the boat pulled up right next to a whale. Everyone was talking excitedly and taking pictures of the whale, but I couldn't have cared less about it. I had one goal: don't throw up. That hour seemed like an eternity. Finally, we headed for shore. I stood on the back deck with about twenty other people, watching the shore approach with increasing desperation. It was so close. Then, about four hundred yards from the dock, seasickness finally overtook me. I leaned over the side of the boat and started vomiting. All twenty people around me gasped in disgust as I emptied all I had into the ocean. It was not a pretty sight. And it didn't end there. I was sick the rest of the day. I will never forget that experience. Sadly, I've never been back on a whale watching excursion.

Our dreams, of course, are so much more significant than a whale watching excursion. But so many of us start out excited about a dream in our hearts, like I was excited about seeing a whale. "I want to be a whale watcher! I want to see a whale up close!" Then we get on our first boat ride in pursuit of that, and instead of seeing a whale, we just puke our guts out. That story then defines the rest of our life. Our inner narrative says, *I tried that once. I wanted to be a whale watcher, but it didn't work out.* And we stop dreaming, stop pursuing what is in our hearts, and stop taking risks. Or some of us don't even make it to the boat. We talk to someone like me, who had a bad experience, and hear, "Oh my, do not go whale watching. I had the worst experience of my life when I tried that." And we let someone else's disappointment stop us from pursuing what's in our hearts.

Too many believers are afraid to take risks because they think, *What if my dream doesn't happen? What if I step out and I pursue who God's called me to be and do what He's called me to do, but I fail in that?* We cannot let the fear of failure stop us from dreaming. If we do not dream, we disengage. Instead of leaning into God, we take a posture of pulling back from Him, which is not the direction we want to be moving. Bill Johnson told me once that the difference between those men and women throughout history who changed the world for God and those who didn't was that the ones who changed the world for God were not afraid to fail for God. We can't be afraid to fail for God. We have to be willing to step out, even when it's scary, because that's what dreamers do.

One of the messages most of us hear at some point is, "Don't get your hopes up." Well-meaning people say this out of pity to give us a dose of reality. They tell young people who have a dream to go to Harvard, "Hey, I know that Harvard is hard to get into. Don't get your hopes up." They treat people as if they're fragile, as if they are going to be crushed by disappointment if their dreams don't happen. Sometimes we even hear this in the church. But 1 Peter 1:3 tells us we've been given a living hope through the resurrection of Jesus. As a people with a living hope, a hope that flows from the victory of resurrection life over death, we are called to get our hopes up after every disappointment. Dreams require that you get your hopes up. Whatever disappointment you may have faced, whatever fear you may have embraced, it is time to hope again. Your dreams depend on it. The body of Christ is to be a place where we hear, "Get your hopes up." Because hope is alive and well!

Step 4: Be Provoked by the Call

When Jonathan looked out at the Israelite soldiers huddling in fear and his father refusing to act, it provoked him. The Israelites had stepped out in their call to drive out their enemies and claim their land, and now they were going to just turn back like cowards? Not cool! They were not acting like the people they were called to be. This spurred Jonathan to do what a true soldier of Israel should have been doing—running with courage toward the battle.

The Bible tells us what the experience of the authentic Christian life should be and the fruit it should produce in our thinking and behavior. At its core, the Christian life is a real, dynamic, interactive relationship with Father, Son, and Holy Spirit that transforms us from the inside out. It is a life full of encounters with the love of God that set us free from sin and shame and bring healing and restoration to our body, soul, and spirit. It is a life of adventure with the Father in which we discover that He fully provides all we need to be successful as we trust Him and walk in obedience. It is a life of partnership in which we get to share His heart to invite the world into this amazing, abundant life. When we're living this life, we look vastly different from the world. The mind of Christ, the heart of the Father, and the fruit of the Spirit become visible and tangible through us.

We are all going to have moments when the Christian life seems to fall short. We're all going to fail to produce the fruit we should be producing. What makes this tragic is when we accept it and settle for a life that falls short of all that God purposed and purchased for us. When life falls short, when others fall short, and when we fall short, it should provoke us, because we know there is more. We should not settle for something less than the fullness of what God has for us. One of the most grievous things happening in the body of Christ today is that a generation of believers is settling for something less than the full, authentic Christian life.

I want you to be dissatisfied. Not ungrateful. Not complaining. Not powerless. But unwilling to accept a life that is less than what God has for you. The call of God on your life should provoke something inside you that causes you to refuse to settle for anything less than all He has called you to be and to do. It's time to start saying, "I'm done settling. God has called me His child, but I've been acting like an orphan. He's promised me a life of freedom and passion, but I've settled for a life of bondage. He's offered me complete security in Him, yet I've settled for a life of insecurity. But not anymore. I want to be who God has called me to be, and experience all He's called me to experience. I was called to change the world."

I pray that God will stir and awaken something in you that refuses to settle, that you would become like Jonathan, not content to sit back in fear, knowing you're called to take on the Philistines. You will never be fully alive or satisfied just sitting there, looking at your call from a distance. It's time to stand up and move toward all that God has called you to be, and to do all that God has called you to do. It's time to step out on the three-mile walk in order to engage the call of God on your life.

2

CHAPTER

—

Do All That Is in Your (Healthy) Heart

I remember the first time I visited Las Vegas to speak at a church. The hotel I stayed at was also a casino. I had seen casinos in movies, but this was the first one I had actually walked through. As I was heading to my room, I walked past the slot machines and was struck by the scene. It looked so different from the extravagant movie shots you see of casinos filled with people laughing, smiling, and having a great time. What I saw were people sitting by themselves, slumped down in chairs, pulling the arms of the slot machines with blank looks on their faces. It was a pretty depressing picture.

Sadly, far too often I see that same blank look on the faces of people in the church. They are sitting there, stalled out, with no real momentum in their lives. This always breaks my heart to see, especially if they are believers in Jesus. They are like King Saul and his six hundred men, unable to face their problems because their hearts have been crushed by intimidating, overwhelming, demoralizing, painful experiences like loss, disappointment, and failure. Life hits us all hard at times. But the Bible makes it clear that Jesus came to give us life, and life to the full (John 10:10). He holds out the hope that nothing can separate us from His love, stop the restorative power of His resurrection life within us, or hold us back from fulfilling all that He has called us to be and to do. The reason I feel sad when I see people stuck in life is because they are missing out on the abundant life God has for them.

One of the greatest passions I have, as a pastor, is to see people thriving in every area of their lives; it's what gets me out of bed in the morning. It brings me such joy to see people get from stalled out to stepping forward into the fullness of the call on their life. However, I don't simply want to see people moving forward. Not all forward movement is the same. Movement can come from two sources of motivation. Some movement is internally driven by a healthy heart, and some is externally driven by circumstances. Both motivators create momentum, but they produce different results.

The difference between internal motivation and external motivation is like the difference between a car and a horse-drawn carriage. It's not difficult to see which one is superior. When cars became widely available, they quickly displaced horse-drawn vehicles—which had been used for centuries—as the dominant form of transportation. With the advent of the internal combustion engine, horsepower moved from outside to inside the vehicle and was vastly multiplied. People also had a greater level of control sitting behind the steering wheel of the car than they did being pulled behind horses, using reins. Once people experienced this way of getting around, there was no going back.

People with internal motivation live in the driver's seat. They have a high level of ownership and responsibility in their choices. They respond more than react. They are powerful in getting where they want to go, with speed and endurance. Externally motivated people, on the other hand, live being dragged or pulled along.

They exhibit a lower level of ownership and responsibility in their choices, typically reacting to things outside them, without much thought or deliberation. They may experience bursts of momentum here and there, but these are usually short-lived and erratic.

The three-mile walk of engaging the call of God requires internal motivation. It's not enough simply to go from stalled out to moving. The only way we will be able to sustain the postures of engagement we looked at in the previous chapter—taking ownership of the call, dreaming about it, counting the cost of pursuing it, and being provoked by it—is with an internal combustion engine. Learning to live from internal motivation is one of the primary things this journey is all about.

Pain or Vision

External motivation is usually connected to our deep human instinct to try to avoid pain at all costs. As most of us discover early in life, pain can be a great motivator to get us unstuck and moving in a direction. Many people we see get busy working hard around us are motivated by painful life circumstances they are trying to escape. A common example is the guy who starts going to marriage counseling and pursuing his wife because things got to a point where she told him, "If things don't change, I'm leaving and I want a divorce." Or there's the guy who starts eating healthy, joins a gym, and makes other radical lifestyle changes because he was diagnosed with diabetes.

When I see someone moving forward in life because of pain, I don't want them to stop moving forward. I'm glad that they're doing something. However, I don't want to see them operating in life solely from a pain motivation. We weren't designed to live our whole lives at the level of avoiding pain. It's been said that we are motivated either by pain or by vision. Pain motivation is all about something we're trying to run away from—who we don't want to be, what we don't want to do. Vision motivation is about something we're trying to get to, something we want—who we want to be, what we want to do, the life we want to live. Vision motivation is always an internally driven reality. I believe that God made us to live pursuing the desires He planted in our hearts rather than running from painful things we want to avoid or being dragged along by circumstances.

The story of the covenants in the Bible shows us how God always intended for us to live. Under the old covenant, people were primarily motivated to keep God's law by the fear of punishment. The old covenant said, "Obey your parents." If the child refused, the response was, "Then we will stone you." In the new covenant, however, the law is written on our hearts (Jer. 31:33). This means that our desire to keep God's law is no longer motivated externally by the fear of punishment; it's now motivated internally by our hearts' desire to live the life God calls us to live. This is why the Holy Spirit takes up residence *inside* us: to empower us to live from the inside out, pursuing His vision and call from a place of desire, not a place of intimidation or coercion.

The goal of living with internal motivation was not introduced in the new covenant, however. In the old covenant, we see God's intention that His people would be motivated by godly love, passion, and vision, not by pain, punishment, guilt, shame, duty, or coercion. God has always wanted His people to be generous and give because we want to, with a willing heart. We see this in both the Old and New Testaments.

> "Take from among you an offering to the LORD. Whoever is of a willing heart, let him bring it as an offering to the LORD: gold, silver, and bronze."
>
> —EXODUS 35:5 NKJV

Let each one give as he purposes in his heart, not grudgingly or of necessity.

—2 CORINTHIANS 9:7 NKJV

As a parent, I know how great it feels when my children do the right thing, not because I made them or they were intimidated into doing it but just because it was in their hearts to do so. If my daughter is mean to her brother, here's how my conversation with her easily could go.

"Apologize to your brother."

"I don't want to."

"Okay, well, you can't drive your car anymore."

"Well, I still don't want to."

"All right, you can't hang out with your friends this weekend."

"Well, I still don't want to."

Then I do the thing I should have done first. "I'm taking your phone away."

"Fine, I'll go apologize."

In a huff, she goes over to her brother and says, "Hey, sorry."

This result does not satisfy me as a parent. I'm not thinking, *It does my heart good to see my daughter apologizing to her brother after I threatened to take away eight things if she didn't.*

It's a different experience for me when my daughter walks over to her brother without prompting and says, "Hey, I'm really sorry. I was mean to you. I'm having a tough day. I love you more than that. You deserve better."

Seeing this makes my heart so happy. I'm texting my wife, "Get in here quick! You've got to see this." We're getting our phones out to film this moment. I'm writing in my journal, *Today was the best day of my life. My daughter apologized on her own because she wanted to.*

43

God shares the same joy when He sees us doing anything He's taught us to do. He is ecstatic when we give cheerfully and generously. But when we say, "Well, fine. Here's my tithe. Here's my offering. God won't be happy with me if I don't," it doesn't delight Him in the same way. It may be better than outright rebellion, but it falls so short of what He desires for us as His kids. There is a joy in giving cheerfully that He wants us to experience, the very joy He experiences as a generous Father who cheerfully gives to us. And we can experience this only when we are motivated by the same things that motivate Him—when our hearts reflect His heart.

A Culture That Prioritizes the External

The Bible makes it clear that everything we do flows from our hearts. Proverbs 4:23 is a verse to which I continually return: "Keep your heart with all diligence, for out of it spring the issues of life" (NKJV). The New Living Translation says, "Guard your heart above all else, for it determines the course of your life." The Hebrew word for heart encompasses everything about your inner world; it's the core of your affections, desires, emotions, imagination, will, convictions, and courage.[1] This internal world defines where your life is headed and how you're engaged in it. This means that both types of motivation—being externally driven by pain avoidance or being internally driven by godly desire and vision—flow from our hearts. However, the first motivation is not healthy, while the second is. If we want to have good motives, we must pay attention to the health of our hearts. Proverbs 4:23 makes it clear that the health of our hearts should be our number one priority.

One of my main concerns when I look at church culture today is that taking care of our hearts doesn't seem to be a priority. Typically, I see that we are prioritizing externals and neglecting our hearts, just like the world. In America, we are not great at prioritizing heart health. Heart-related issues are the number one cause of death, surpassing cancer and other illnesses. Though many heart issues have genetic causes, our lifestyles determine how these develop and are expressed in our lives. Theoretically, we have the knowledge and wealth to create the healthiest lifestyles of any generation in human history, thanks to our access to good nutrition, exercise, meaningful work, leisure time, and many other resources. Instead the American lifestyle has two main stereotypes. We are either passive consumers who live sedentary lives, or we are hyperdriven, stressed-out producers obsessed with external achievements. Both lifestyles are driven by pain avoidance. Both neglect the heart, focus on externals, and put us on the short track to physical, mental, emotional, spiritual, and relational breakdown.

I wish I could say these stereotypes don't apply in the American church (and to the church in other places around the world). But in general, I see us just as preoccupied with pain avoidance and externals as the culture around us, and I see us generating the same producer-consumer dynamic.

We have a culture in the church that is creating leaders who are producers. They are not sitting on the sideline waiting for life to happen; they are moving and getting stuff done. They are building ministries and structures to meet people's needs and make a difference in the world. These are not bad things. But all too often, they are not internally motivated by healthy hearts, and eventually their unhealthy heart motivations catch up with them. Over the years, I have watched many pastors and leaders in the body of Christ, both young and old, end up in moral failure, burnout, or both. Nothing is more grieving or sobering to me than to watch gifted men and women who love God fall apart because of unhealthy heart issues and hurt their families, communities, and churches.

Just as grieving is that we seem to have a culture in the church that makes excuses for unhealthy patterns and behaviors that lead to this, because we value results above all else.

Recently I was at a gathering of pastors during which we held a men-only session to have an open and honest conversation about some of the challenges we were facing in our lives and leadership. I really wanted to go after the question of whether we were prioritizing our internal health and motivations or making excuses and allowing unhealthy things to remain in our hearts. When it was my turn to speak, I said, "I think we, as leaders, have our priorities out of order. I think we are putting externals before our internal health, and I think this is setting us up for burnout and other bad consequences. Do you agree, and what can we do about this?"

In the course of that discussion, one of the pastors there, a dear friend of mine and a wonderful pastor and leader, said something quite vulnerable and profound. He admitted, "I am afraid that if I get healthy, I will lose my ambition." He had the self-awareness to see and recognize that his motives were unhealthy, yet he didn't want to let them go. Why? Because they were tied to a certain identity and definition of success that he couldn't imagine living without. He was a producer, and that was the thing others celebrated and rewarded him for. People weren't impressed by his internal world; they were impressed by what they saw him producing. If he chose internal health in his life and didn't appear as driven or stopped achieving certain numbers, then people probably wouldn't be as impressed and the applause would die down.

It was sobering for me to consider my friend's words. I know him to be a humble, gifted leader who sincerely loves Jesus. I thought, *If leaders like him are struggling to run fully after heart health, then I know that less-mature leaders are prioritizing it even less.*

Not everyone reading this book is a pastor or on staff at a

church. But it's important to understand the culture we are creating in the church and how it affects not only the leaders but every one of us. We take this unhealthy mindset, and it shows up in other areas of our lives. When producers are leading our churches, it sends the message to people that they can become one of two things—a consumer or another producer. Consumers are believers who are allowed to stay in a state of spiritual immaturity because the producers keep doing for them what they should be learning to do for themselves. To use the earlier illustration, they are confined to driving around in horse-drawn carriages because they are never given the chance to change to a vehicle with an internal combustion engine.

My oldest daughter, Ellianna, didn't crawl until she was ten months old and didn't walk until she was fifteen months old. When our second daughter, Raya, came along, she surprised us all by crawling at six months and walking at nine months. Though I know it's common for each child to develop at their own pace, I also think one of the things that affected this process with our daughters was the shift in our style of parenting from the first to the second child. With Elli, all she had to do was make a sound, and we rushed over and picked her up. "Are you okay? Do you need something? What can I do for you? I'll pick you up and move you." I'm sure she was thinking, *Why would I walk? My parents will come pick me up and move me where I want to go. I can get from point A to point B just fine.* By the time Raya came along, we were much more relaxed. We had learned to discern which sounds and cries deserved our immediate attention and which ones she would probably quit making if we let her figure out what to do or get distracted by something else. We gave her more opportunities to struggle and develop skills in the process.

Healthy leadership, like healthy parenting, provides structure to meet people's needs, but always with the goal of helping them mature from dependence to independence and interdependence. Unhealthy leadership keeps people in a state of dependence. The church is full of people who are saved and going to heaven but are deeply unhealthy and immature. Instead of teaching them to take care of their hearts and become healthy, mature, and internally motivated, however, we create structures around them that just pick them up and move them.

I believe that much of the structure we have built in the church comes from a good heart and a sincere desire to help people. I don't know any leader or pastor who wants to build something that keeps people immature. Nor do I know any Christian who wants to remain immature. The problem comes in when we don't realize that the culture around us in the world has crept in and influences what we do in the church. In America, and in much of the world, we live in a consumer society. Everything around us is tailored to get us to spend money at a particular business. When businesses compete for our money, they want to remove all obstacles and struggles in our path to make life as easy as possible for us, which is appealing. Entire marketing campaigns have been built around an "easy button." The business is trying to make things as easy as possible and remove all struggle so you will choose them over another establishment. A coffee shop realizes one day that it's a hassle for people to have to get out of their car, walk in, stand in line, order coffee, walk back to their car, and drive away. So they put in a drive-through to make it easier for the customer. They just made it easier for those with busy lives. Now people are choosing their coffee shop over another coffee shop not because the coffee is better but because it's easier. Businesses are building systems and structures to make it easier for you so that you will choose them and spend your money there.

I love that people are trying to make my life easier, and I have no problem with consumerism—until it comes into the church. Trying to make the Christian life easier for people does not always help them. Many leaders are trying to make things as easy as possible for people by building structures and systems where they can participate in community, serving, giving, praying, taking care of the poor, and the other things with minimal effort. I believe the intention is good, but the result is that we create churchgoers who are dependent on outside structure, rather than internal conviction, to motivate them.

The goal of the church is not to get people's money, and the goal of the kingdom is not to make their lives easier. The goal is to connect people to God and mature them. Maturity, by nature, requires struggle and hard work. As Bill Johnson says, "Gifts are free, but maturity is expensive." The gift of salvation is free. The gifts of the Spirit are free. Everything we receive from God is freely given and can only be freely received. But walking out our salvation, growing our character, and learning to maturely operate in the gifts God has given us is costly.

There is a story that beautifully illustrates this. A man found a cocoon of an emperor moth and took it home so he could watch the moth come out. One day, a small opening appeared in the cocoon. The man sat and watched the moth for several hours as it struggled to force its body through the little hole. Then the man noticed that the moth had stopped struggling and appeared to be stuck. He concluded that it had gotten as far as it could and couldn't go any farther, so in his kindness, he decided to help the moth. With a pair of scissors, he snipped off the remaining bit of the cocoon, and the moth emerged with ease. However, its body was swollen and its wings were shriveled. The man watched it, expecting to see its wings expand and its body contract to normal size, but neither happened! The little moth spent the rest of its life crawling around with a swollen body and shriveled wings, unable to fly. What the man in his haste had not understood was that the restricting cocoon and the struggle required for the moth to get through the tiny opening was nature's way of forcing fluid from the moth's body into its wings so it would be ready for flight once it achieved freedom from the cocoon. Freedom and flight would come only after the struggle. Depriving the moth of this struggle, the man unwittingly deprived it of health and its natural body.

Please hear me on this. I do not have a problem with structure or systems that serve people. My only point is that we sometimes don't realize that we are creating a culture in the church that keeps people dependent on external motivations rather than moving them into a place of internal motivation. Allowing struggle is part of that; it's what forces people to develop the maturity and endurance to do this three-mile walk well.

There's a word for the culture that prioritizes the external over the internal: *religion*. Religion cares only about your external world. I grew up in a religious environment. My hometown gets hot in the summers; it is consistently over 100 degrees Fahrenheit in the summer and sometimes will reach as high as 120 degrees. When I was in middle school, I went to Sunday school one summer morning wearing shorts. Almost immediately after I walked into class, someone looked at me and asked sarcastically, "Oh, you're wearing shorts to church?" On another occasion years ago, I was invited to speak at a church and brought a friend with me. The friend happened to be wearing a baseball hat when we walked in the sanctuary. Moments after we walked in, an usher approached my friend and sternly told him he had to take his hat off in church. I understand that churches have different cultures around appropriate dress, and it's a matter of good manners to honor these; I'm not advocating bad manners or disrespect. I also understand that in California we have a casual culture, and it shows in how we do church. But it's not because I live in California that I don't care what you wear to church; it's because Jesus doesn't care what you wear to church. He cares way more about what is happening in your heart than about the clothes you are wearing when you show up on Sunday. When we care more about correcting minor issues of appearance than about the issues of the heart, we send the message that how things look on the outside is more important than what's inside.

This is a problem because religion is 100 percent opposed to the kingdom of God. Jesus insisted that what is going on inside us is a million times more important than what's going on externally, and saved His harshest criticism for those who prioritized the external over the internal. When He confronted the Pharisees, who represented religious culture, He said, "Now you Pharisees make the outside of the cup and dish clean, but your inward part is full of greed and wickedness" (Luke 11:39 NKJV). It's possible to look amazing on the outside and be rotten inside, and religion is satisfied with that. This is exactly what religion is: good actions performed with bad motives. That's why it wants us to focus on the pretty outside instead of the rotten inside. But Jesus is not satisfied with it, for good reason: He knows it will ultimately destroy us. If we want to align with His kingdom, we must prioritize the internal before the external and focus on getting our hearts healthy.

Tending Our Internal Garden

The Bible says to keep our hearts with all diligence. The word diligence means "careful and persistent work or effort." Your internal world is like a garden you must be diligent in tending. If you aren't familiar with the demands of gardening, let me enlighten you: it requires *a lot* of intentionality. I learned this from watching my wife, SeaJay, who loves to garden. She finds life in planting things, caring for them, and seeing them grow. Her dream is to live on a farm in the country, where she can have a huge garden and as many animals as she desires. For now, we live in the suburbs, so she's slowly but surely turning our back yard into a suburban farm. So far, we are raising bunnies, chickens, and a decent-size garden of flowers, herbs, and vegetables.

Recently I bought SeaJay a small greenhouse to aid in her back-yard farm endeavors. She was so excited to get a batch of seedlings growing in there. We bought several bags of soil pods and many packets of seeds, which SeaJay carefully planted in trays. We were supposed to see the seeds sprouting within a few days. However, a full week passed and nothing appeared. Finally, we accepted the truth: our seeds had not germinated. The next thing to do was to figure out why. Eventually we discovered the problem. We had mistakenly covered the trays, which doubled the heat on the seeds and cooked them. Who knew?

Gardening takes diligence. You can't just approach it casually or flippantly. You've got to prepare the soil so the plants have room and nutrients to grow. You need to plant the plants where they'll get the right amount of sunlight; some plants need more sun, and others need less. You've got to give them water, but not too much or too little. Then you've got to make sure there are no bugs or snails, and if there are deer in the area, you have to build fences around the garden to keep them out. Each season of the year requires different tasks to keep the garden healthy, even when nothing is growing in it. And when things are growing, they need regular attention. You can't go on vacation or ignore your garden for a few weeks if you want to see good results. Gardening takes diligence.

Likewise, keeping the garden of our hearts requires us to be diligent in meeting specific needs in order for our hearts to function as they were designed. On the physical level, the heart is responsible for circulating the blood in our bodies, providing them with oxygen and nutrients while removing carbon dioxide and other waste. To do this well, our hearts need things like good nutrition, sleep, exercise, and the right kind and degree of stress. That's why if you ignore your physical heart, it becomes costly. Similarly, on the emotional and spiritual level, a healthy heart produces healthy emotions and beliefs, which fuel godly desires and vision to motivate us. To produce healthy emotions and beliefs, we must feed our hearts a steady diet of truth and love, and remove anything that produces unhealthy beliefs and emotions.

When we get to the root of issues of the heart that are unhealthy —bitterness, offense, pride, anger, disappointment, unbelief, and insecurity—we find that they are all based on some form of fear. When I'm trying to help someone who is struggling, or when I'm struggling myself, the question that typically gets to the bottom of the issue fastest is, "What am I scared of right now?" Naming the fear—the fear of failure, of not being accepted, of not being taken care of, of being less than, of not being loved, of loss, whatever it may be—brings the issue into clear focus.

The good news is that just as all heart issues have the same root, they also have the same antidote. First John 4:18 tells us that perfect love is what casts out fear, and Romans 5:5 tells us that it is the Holy Spirit who pours out this love in our hearts. Remember, in the new covenant, He is the one who trains, equips, and empowers us to live from our hearts. The health of our hearts is very important to Him, which is why He is constantly encountering our hearts with His love to drive out fear and make us whole. If we have bitterness or offense, His love helps us to forgive. If we have loss and disappointment, His love comforts us and restores our hope. If we have insecurity, His love brings acceptance, worthiness, and confidence. Our role in keeping our internal garden healthy is really just learning to continually invite the Holy Spirit to show us where fear is at work and allowing Him to perfect His love there.

We Need Those Who Speak to Our Hearts

This brings up the point that becoming heart healthy is a journey we cannot take alone. While we are individually responsible for the health of our hearts, we cannot achieve it by ourselves. We need the Holy Spirit's love and the love of the Spirit-filled body of Christ to help us tend our internal gardens and drive fear away. This is why I am so passionate about calling the body of Christ corporately to focus on the health of our internal world; we need to do this together if we're going to make the transition from external motivation to internal motivation, from pain to vision, from unhealthy to healthy.

Jonathan didn't take his three-mile journey alone. He told his armor-bearer what was in his heart and allowed him to weigh in on the decision. The armor-bearer knew that Jonathan's desire was coming from a healthy place, so he said, "Do all that's in your heart. I am here with you according to your heart." This gives us a glimpse into the relationship these two friends had. They weren't simply master and servant; they spoke to one another on a heart level.

We need to be walking with the Holy Spirit and with people who know us and speak to us on this heart level, because no matter where we are on our journey, none of us has achieved perfect health. We still have heart issues we haven't dealt with. There are still fear-based motives in us we are unaware of until situations test us and expose them. One of the main things the Holy Spirit is doing as we engage His call on our lives is leading us into situations in which our hearts are exposed so we can see where we have mixed motives and adjust. He wants us to live from vision and desire, but our vision and desires don't yet line up with His vision and desires for our lives. To get our hearts healthy, we must go through a process of aligning our hearts with His.

We all have mixed motives in the gardens of our hearts. We want to love God with all our heart, soul, mind, and strength, but we want to protect ourselves and hold on to fear and not trust that He's really good. We want to love our neighbors as ourselves, but we struggle with comparison, jealousy, and shame. We want to believe in the dreams and desires God put in our hearts, but we wrestle with the fear of man and fear of failure. When the Holy Spirit or another believer shows us these weeds in the gardens of our hearts, it isn't to shame us. It's just to show us that we have some things to pull out so we can get healthy, some areas where we need love to be perfected in our internal world.

When we're walking with the Holy Spirit and other believers, there's protection as our hearts are exposed. They help us see issues early so we can deal with them before they take over our internal gardens. When we're isolated and not walking in relationship with people who can see and speak to our hearts, however, we're in danger.

One of the dangers I see is that often the mixed motives in people's hearts make it difficult to recognize the difference between the dreams God is awakening in them and fantasies or wishful thinking rooted in fear. This is a wall I often run into when I'm trying to disciple people in pursuing their dreams. As they pursue what they think is a God dream, it becomes clear that this dream doesn't match up with the favor or gifting in their life. Someone may have a dream of being a worship leader. Their fantasy is that they'll end up on a national stage and record albums, but they haven't been gifted with a voice or talent on that level. If they take voice lessons and practice hard and improve, they will be able to lead worship in some capacity somewhere, but the big platform or career is not what God has gifted them or given them favor to do. Someone else may have a dream to be on a leadership team. Their fantasy is to be the head leader, but their gifting is better suited to a supporting role on the team.

The challenge for me, as a pastor, is to speak to these people's hearts in a way that doesn't shut them down but also doesn't feed an unhealthy fantasy that will end in disappointment and disillusionment. This goes well when the person is open to letting others speak to their heart, and badly when they are not. I am for people and what's in their hearts. I never want to crush people or their dreams. I also recognize that many times we desire something not because God has called us to it but because we think it will satisfy an unhealthy desire. In the example of being a worship leader or a head leader, that might be coming from a place where we long for acceptance and see those roles as what people value most. We want that because we want to be valued. I don't think that's the case all the time, but we need to be honest and aware of what is going on inside us and what is motivating us.

Another common way we get misaligned with God in pursuing our dreams is that we stumble over certain expectations about how and when they will happen. I remember praying one morning in my midtwenties and feeling frustrated because my destiny wasn't happening as quickly as I wanted it to. Suddenly, in the midst of my prayer, the Holy Spirit showed me that I was praying as if God owed me my destiny, as if I deserved it. But God doesn't owe me my destiny. I did not die on the cross for Him. He gave His life for me, and I owe Him everything. I had allowed an attitude of entitlement to creep into my relationship with God and what I believed I deserved from Him. When I realized that, my prayer changed. I simply wanted to be obedient and do my assignment. The timing was up to Him. The moment my heart got aligned with His, my frustration disappeared.

We're Called to Live from Healthy Hearts

The only way we will take this three-mile walk successfully is if we have healthy hearts. Saul and Jonathan show us the profound difference between a healthy heart and an unhealthy heart. If you read the life of Jonathan, you see a heart that was healthy. He was secure, humble, courageous, and faithful. He wasn't driven by fear or the desire to avoid pain. Saul was a different story. He was deeply insecure, jealous, and full of the fear of man. It was not unhealthy Saul who took off on the three-mile walk. It was Jonathan, who could be trusted to do all that was in his heart, because he had a healthy heart.

God cares about what is in your heart. My prayer is that you will be able to do all that is in your heart, but only your healthy heart, because that is aligned with the desires and vision of God for your life. It may seem counterintuitive that after taking the first step forward to engage the call on our lives, the next step is to turn inward. But again, not all forward movement is equal. We need to keep moving forward on this journey while increasingly making sure that that movement is coming from a healthy place. This takes diligence; it's hard work to prioritize our hearts in a culture that is constantly pressuring us to listen to fear, care about externals, and operate as immature producers or consumers instead of mature sons and daughters. But the more our internal world gets healthy—the more we experience the power of life driven by vision and desires that align with God's heart for us—the more powerful and free we become to be and do what He's called us to be and do. It's what we're made for, and we must settle for nothing less.

MILE 1

-

HOLINESS

MANY PEOPLE THINK WE BECOME HOLY
BY THE ERADICATION OF SOMETHING
EVIL WITHIN. NO, WE BECOME HOLY
BY BEING SEPARATED UNTO GOD.

—Watchman Nee

3

CHAPTER

—

The Few Who Raise Their Hand

One of the great lies people believe is that there is a hierarchy of calls, either that some people are called by God and others aren't or that some people's calls are more important than others. Typically, the lie is that those in professional Christian ministry—with titles such as pastor, missionary, worship leader—or those with more talent, gifting, and influence are called or have higher calls. It suggests that those who preach or sing songs are more important than someone who answers phones or that those performing on big platforms with big visibility and impact are more significant than those doing small things hidden from most of the world. But every believer in Jesus has a call from God, whatever your talent or gifting, wherever you live and work, and whomever you serve and influence, whether inside or outside the walls of the church.

What separates you is not the call on your life, because every believer has a call. What separates you is your response to that call. This is what separated Jonathan and his armor-bearer from King Saul and the rest of the Israelite army. Every one of those six hundred men—not to mention the rest of the men of Israel—had been called to defeat the Philistines and establish righteousness in the land. Only two of them responded to the call in that moment, while the rest of them were content to sit and wait. Jonathan and his armor-bearer's response to the call, not the call itself, was what separated them from the rest.

RSVP

Our response has always mattered to God. His sovereignty does not exclude human responsibility. Many people believe that God's sovereignty means He is going to do what He wants to do when He wants to do it, and we play no part in that equation. But Scripture shows us that what God wants to do, in His sovereignty, is to partner with men and women to accomplish His plans and purposes in the earth. This was the intention He expressed in the creation story in Genesis 1 and 2. The fall damaged that partnership, but God's grand plan in human history has always been to restore it. Every move of God in the Bible begins with God pursuing individuals and inviting them into partnership.

The burning bush Moses encountered is a great example of one of these God invitations. After the people of Israel spent four hundred years in slavery, the time had come for God to set them free from the bondage of Egypt, just as He had promised to their ancestor Abraham (Gen. 15:13–14). His plan was to have Moses lead His people out of bondage and into the promised land. But God first needed to meet with Moses and speak to him about the part he would play. So God sent Moses an invitation in the form of a burning bush.

The nature of invitations is that they require a response. Many invitations we receive to birthday parties, weddings, or other events have "RSVP" on them. These initials come from the French phrase *Répondez s'il vous plaît*, which means "Please respond." God's invitation to Moses required him to turn aside to find out what was going on with this bush that was on fire but not consumed.

> Now Moses was tending the flock of Jethro his father-in-law, the priest of Midian. And he led the flock to the back of the desert, and came to Horeb, the mountain of God. And the Angel of the LORD appeared to him in a flame of fire from the midst of a bush. So he looked, and behold, the bush was burning with fire, but the bush was not consumed. Then Moses said, "I will now turn aside and see this great sight, why the bush does not burn."
>
> So when the LORD saw that he turned aside to look, God called to him from the midst of the bush and said, "Moses, Moses!"
>
> And he said, "Here I am."
>
> Then He said, "Do not draw near this place. Take your sandals off your feet, for the place where you stand is holy ground."
>
> —EXODUS 3:1–5 NKJV

Notice, only when the Lord saw that Moses had turned aside did He speak to him from the midst of the bush. The burning bush was not the encounter; it was simply the invitation. Moses had to respond to the invitation, and then God spoke to him.

We find this pattern of invitation and response throughout Scripture. In 2 Kings 9, Elisha commissioned one of the sons of the prophets to anoint Jehu king of Israel. God was about to use Jehu to end the wicked reign of Jezebel. But Elisha gave the prophet specific instructions about how first to invite Jehu to receive this anointing: "Now when you arrive at that place, look there for Jehu the son of Jehoshaphat, the son of Nimshi, and go in and make him rise up from among his associates, and take him to an inner room" (2 Kings 9:2 NKJV). When the prophet arrived at the house where Jehu was staying, he said, "I have a message for you, Commander" (v. 5). Only after Jehu had responded to the invitation and risen up to follow him into the house did the prophet deliver the message and anoint him king.

Each of Jesus' disciples received an invitation that required a response: they had to leave everything behind to follow Him. When the time came for Jesus to end His earthly ministry, He explained to the disciples that a transition was coming: they would receive power from on high when God poured out the Spirit. But again, their response was required: they were to wait in Jerusalem for this to occur (Acts 1:4–5). They responded to that invitation and prayed together in an upper room for ten days. On the day of Pentecost, the Holy Spirit was poured out (Acts 2:1–4).

We find this pattern of invitation and response again and again throughout Scripture, right up till the final book of the Bible, where Jesus announced, "Behold, I stand at the door and knock. If anyone hears My voice and opens the door, I will come in to him and dine with him, and he with Me" (Rev. 3:20 NKJV). Jesus invites us to dine and fellowship with Him, but we must respond and open the door.

God's invitations are not always loud. Many times they are subtle and quiet, heard only by those whose hearts are tender and who have ears to hear. Even the burning bush was not as dramatic as it sounds. In Sunday school as a kid, I always pictured the burning bush as this massive bonfire in the desert. But scholars believe that the bush was the lowliest of shrubs, not big at all. It required Moses to pay attention and keep his heart tender to the invitation of God.

Are there exceptions to this pattern? Yes. There are times when God speaks before waiting for our response; Paul on the road to

Damascus is one example. In His grace, He will sometimes interrupt people to get their attention when they cannot hear Him or are ignoring Him. Once He has their attention, though, their response to whatever He says is still required.

We find this same pattern throughout church history. Every awakening, revival, outpouring of the Spirit, or move of God is connected to individuals who responded to the call of God. These men and women weren't randomly chosen; every one of them ended up playing a role in the move of God because they responded to God's invitation to partner with Him. Too often we see only the part of the story where the breakthrough happened and don't connect it to the moments before the breakthrough—often years before—when these individuals responded to the invitation of God.

The Welsh Revival is widely recognized as one of the greatest revivals in history. It began in 1904 and lasted about nine months. In that short time, one hundred thousand people were saved and added to the church. From Wales, the revival ignited a worldwide movement that is still impacting the world today. Much of the church globally can trace their roots back to the Welsh Revival.

The leading figure in the Welsh Revival was a young Welshman named Evan Roberts. He was twenty-six years old when he became God's catalyst to release this awakening across Wales and the nations of the earth. But God's invitation had come to him ten years earlier, when he was just a teenager. God had stirred Roberts's heart to believe for revival in Wales, and he had responded by giving himself to prayer, fasting, and reading the Word. By the time the revival broke out, Roberts had been faithfully partnering with God for a decade in response to the call.

A more recent outpouring, the Brownsville Revival, was a significant move of God marked by repentance, salvations, and tangible hunger for God. It began on Father's Day 1995, when an evangelist named Steve Hill came to preach in Pensacola, Florida. The revival lasted for five years, with nightly meetings Tuesday through Saturday. People were so hungry to experience the presence of God that they lined up before dawn to get into the meetings. Some even camped overnight. Within the first year, 1.7 million people had visited the meetings, and 108,000 people had responded to an altar call.

But this outpouring did not just show up out of nowhere. Two years prior to that Father's Day in 1995, the pastor of Brownsville Assembly of God, John Kilpatrick, was moved to pray for revival. He called the church to prayer, and they turned their regular Sunday night services into prayer meetings where they pressed in for what God had awakened in their hearts. Their response to God's invitation prepared the way for Him to move as He'd moved them to pray.

Few Are Chosen

A common element in all these stories is that every move of God begins with Him inviting just one or a few people to partner with Him. When people draw attention to this fact, they often quote Matthew 22:14: "Many are called, but few are chosen" (NKJV). This was one of those verses that used to frustrate me as a young man. I was so passionate for God and dreamed of being used by Him to change the world. But this verse seemed to suggest there was a chance I could be called by God but not chosen. I remember praying, "God, I don't understand why many are called but few are chosen. I don't want to be in the 'many' category; I want to be in the 'few' category."

Eventually I studied that verse in its context. Jesus was telling a parable about a king who sent servants out to invite guests to his son's wedding feast. The first group of guests repeatedly refused to come; some even beat and killed a few of the servants. So the king angrily removed them from the guest list, sent the servants out to invite anyone and everyone they found to come to the wedding feast, and everyone who accepted the invitation got to join the party. Jesus concluded the parable with, "Many are called, but few are chosen." Looking at the context, I finally understood that those who were chosen were simply those who accepted their invitation and responded to the call. The reason many are called but few are chosen is because the call requires a response, and only a few RSVP'd and showed up for the party.

There's more going on in this parable that we need to understand, however. On the surface, it seems strange that a king would have so much trouble getting people to show up at a big party. But the wedding feast is a symbol for covenant relationship. Even today, we don't invite just anyone to our weddings; hopefully, we invite those with whom we have important connections, people who have invested in our lives in a significant way. This was certainly the case in first-century Jewish culture, in which weddings were not just about two people committing to one another; they were about an entire community committing to partner with the merging of two families. Attending a wedding feast showed that you were committed to these important relationships, while refusing to attend showed that they weren't important to you. It was one of those lines in the sand that told everyone whether you were true covenant friends.

I often joke that in my life one of those relational lines in the sand is moving day. There are few things I want to do less than moving. I don't like the entire process, from start to finish. And for some reason, moving days always seem to fall on one of the hottest days in the middle of summer in California, when the last thing you want to be doing is working hard loading up vans and U-Hauls and awkwardly maneuvering furniture through doorways that never seem to be wide enough. Then, after all that, you have to unpack and set up the house.

But what I dislike even more than moving is helping other people move. The problem I run into, however, is that helping people seems to be the true sign of friendship. If you want to find out who your real friends are, tell people that you're moving on the hottest Saturday in the summer and ask for their help. The ones who show up are your real friends. I can just see how it would go if I walked up to a group of my friends and said, "Hey, on Saturday I'm going to be moving. Can anybody help?" Immediately I will see heads lowering and faces turning to avoid eye contact as people try to think of some excuse, praying that they will remember some previous commitment that coming Saturday. Then one guy will finally raise his hand and say, "Yeah, I'll help you." I look at him and say, "All right. I choose you."

This is how it works in the kingdom. Jesus invites us to partner with Him: "Will you follow Me? Will you be a leader in your generation? Will you be a good husband and a godly father? A good wife and godly mother? Will you stand for the truth of the kingdom? Will you change the world around you? Will you serve and lay your life down to see people encounter My love? Will you give yourself to see My purposes fulfilled on the earth?" Many people look away and think of excuses, not wanting to respond to Jesus' invitation. But then there's a handful who raise their hands and say, "Yes, Jesus, I will answer the call. I will follow You. I will be a leader in my generation. I will pursue who You have called me to be and press in for what You have called me to do." And Jesus says, "All right. Then I choose you." The reason why only a few are chosen is because only a few raise their hands. Will you be one who raises your hand?

Two Fears

My heart has always been to see people fully engaged in pursuing the call of God on their lives, whether it is teenagers reaching their campus, young adults engaging justice issues in their day, or adults understanding how where they are and what they are doing is a vital part of the plan of God. I have seen many who have engaged their call and have made a difference, while others have not. I always wondered what the difference was between those who did something for God and those who didn't. Many have sat under the same teaching, learned the same things, and shared similar experiences. Finally, the truth dawned on me. It was very simple. The only difference between those who did something for God and those who didn't was that those who did something for God *did something*. It may seem obvious, but what separates you is the simple act of moving forward to engage the call of God in some way, no matter how small.

So what about the people who don't do something? What holds them back? In my observation, there are two fears that hold us back from engaging our call: *the fear of failure* and *the fear of rejection*. When we find ourselves crippled by indecision, unable or unwilling to move forward, these are typically the fears keeping us stuck.

The fear of failure sounds like, "What if I mess up?" In our minds, messing up means losing something valuable and being devastated or ruined by that loss. We want to avoid these painful experiences at all costs, so whenever we're faced with a decision where we must risk failure, this fear often shows up, sometimes to a paralyzing degree.

Years ago I was wrestling with a decision that could affect my future and family in a significant way because it involved moving to a new city and joining a new ministry. The more I wrestled, the more anxious I became. I felt increasingly desperate not to make the wrong decision, because I thought that if I made the wrong decision, it would take the call of God on my life off course and mess it up, or at best slow it down. I did not want to make the wrong decision.

One day, I felt so overwhelmed with the stakes of this decision that I went out to walk around the neighborhood and pray. Midway through the walk, the Lord interrupted my anxious prayers with this simple statement: *Banning, you're not that big.*

It stopped me in my tracks. *What do You mean by that?* I asked.

You're not that big, He repeated. *You think that one decision is going to ruin My call on your life? You're giving yourself way too much credit. You aren't big enough to mess up the plans I have for you by one decision.*

When we allow the fear of failure to keep us from moving forward, we are acting as if failure were more powerful than God. We must believe God is greater than our failures. When we do, here's what we discover: as long as we are moving forward with Him, we will be successful. Yes, we can make mistakes, but we won't do anything fatal that will disqualify ourselves from our calling. The only way we disqualify ourselves is by repeatedly refusing to move forward with Him. And God is extremely gracious about giving us many chances to change course, even when there is rebellion in our hearts. Just ask Jonah. If we are doing our best to follow Jesus, stay humble in community, and do what He is asking of us, then we don't need to worry so much about making the wrong decision.

This doesn't mean we shouldn't use wisdom and discernment to try to make the best decisions possible. But wisdom and discernment are gained through experience, through stepping out to engage what God has put in our hearts, seeing what happens, learning from it, adjusting, and continuing to step out with Him. Making mistakes is part of that learning process. Should we be careless or willfully make mistakes? Of course not. But even when we're trying our best, we will make mistakes, and we can be confident that God is right there to use those mistakes to help us grow. The more we experience this, the freer we become to move forward without fear.

One of the most freeing things I've learned on this three-mile walk is that God is really good at opening doors and equally good at closing doors. We pray often for open doors but don't understand the power of a closed door. He is faithful to give us green lights, yellow lights, and red lights at the right time. He also brings us wisdom through others, which is why it's so important for us to receive counsel and make decisions in community. Our job is to move forward, trusting that He will bring us what we need at the right time to make us successful. We must not allow the fear of failure to keep us on the sideline of the call God has for us.

The fear of rejection is the other fear that holds us back from responding to the call of God. The need to be accepted and belong is basic to our humanity. We find safety, identity, comfort, and purpose in our connections with other people, and anything that threatens these can seem devastating to us. When faced with a decision that risks disappointing, displeasing, or even just departing from the important people in our life (or even those we do not know but from whom we want acceptance), we often battle with this fear.

When I was a youth pastor, there was a young girl in our church whose heart was awakened to see abortion end in her generation. She felt like she was supposed to pray and go after that issue in our city, so she asked a bunch of her friends if they would gather with her weekly to pray in a quiet place near the abortion clinic. A month or two after she had started her prayer meetings, I checked in with her to ask how it was going.

"Well, no one was really into it," she told me. "A few people showed up one time, and then no one really wanted to come anymore."

"So you've stopped praying?" I asked.

"Yeah," she admitted.

"Hey, I know it's hard to go alone," I said. "But God put this in your heart. Even if nobody else goes, I think you're supposed to go. Don't wait for someone else. You don't need a crowd to go with you to respond to what God is calling you to do." And she did. She responded and continued to pray. Even when no one else showed up, she was faithful to pursue what God had placed in her heart. As a youth pastor, I could not have been more proud of her.

Many of us feel safety in numbers, secure when someone else is taking the lead and showing us where to go. But behind this hides a deep insecurity that apart from the crowd, we don't have what it takes. It's the flip side of the lie behind our fear of failure. We exaggerate our ability to mess things up, but diminish the significance and impact we can have when we partner with God.

One of the reasons moves of God start with only one or a few people is that He needs only a few to respond to His invitation. This is the nature of movements: they always start with the few instead of the many. In his book *The Tipping Point*, Malcolm Gladwell argues that social trends, ideas, and movements spread through culture just like viruses spread. One of the principles behind how this works is what he calls "The Law of the Few." Basically, only 20 percent of the people in a social group are doing the work to influence the other 80 percent. It begins with one person or a handful of pioneers who create something new—say, a fashion style—and then a few other people who promote it or pass it along. This is how you go from having a handful of people in one neighborhood in New York City start wearing a certain piece of clothing to it catching on like wildfire till masses around the nation are all wearing the same thing.

The same pattern applies with revival. Revival doesn't begin with the masses; it always begins with the few. No revival ever launched in a stadium full of people with hundreds of thousands of salvations. Every revival started with a few people who responded to God's invitation by doing something to engage what He was calling them to do—a handful of college students who decided to commit to the mission field, individuals who committed to pray and fast every day for a season, or a group of young people who gathered in a barn to seek God. Out of these simple acts of obedience, God birthed movements that changed history.

If we find ourselves paralyzed by indecision or scrambling for excuses not to engage our call, chances are that we are under the influence of the fear of failure or the fear of rejection. It is critical that we face these fears and move forward. Both fears are based on lies. Failure is not fatal. We're not big enough to mess up our call. Rejection won't destroy us. We are significant, and this shines all the more when we are willing to step out from the crowd and do what God's invited us to do, alone or with the few.

And then there's the third lie, the lie that if we listen to our fears, we'll be protected. But we won't be. Attempting to live without ever risking failure or rejection is the most dangerous and costly path we can take.

Counting the Cost

The choice not to respond to God's call is not a neutral choice. I once watched an episode of a Bear Grylls TV show in which he was teaching people what to do if they ever get lost in the wilderness. In so many words, he said, "One of the worst things you can do if you're lost is not to do anything. Some people die in the wilderness because they just don't want to make the wrong decision, so therefore, they make no decision." This was true of an entire generation of Israelites who died in the wilderness after being miraculously delivered from slavery in Egypt. God brought them to the promised land and explained how He would partner with them to drive out the people in the land and establish their borders. However, the people listened to the reports of the spies and were paralyzed by fear. Their refusal to respond to God's invitation condemned them to die in the wilderness, costing them the greatest gift they had ever been offered.

The same is true in our lives. Life is not a choice between a safe and easy path and a hard and dangerous path. It is a choice between trusting God or trusting anything or anyone else. Both are risky. Both are dangerous. Both are difficult. Both are costly. But one path—partnering with God and becoming who we were created to be—leads us to the greatest prize in the universe, while the other leads to destruction.

Jesus was constantly confronting people about this issue of where they were putting their trust. One shocking example: His conversation with the crowds after feeding the five thousand. As Bible scholars tell us, that number refers only to the men present; they estimate that if women and children had also been counted, somewhere around fifteen thousand people gathered to hear Jesus' teaching and partook of His miraculous meal of loaves and fish. Afterward, huge numbers of this group were ready to join Jesus' movement. "After the people saw the sign Jesus performed, they began to say, 'Surely this is the Prophet who is to come into the world'" (John 6:14). I, like most speakers and leaders I know, consider being able to gather fifteen thousand people for a conference and getting a positive response from them to be a huge success. We might assume that after this remarkable gathering, Jesus would excitedly welcome this multitude as His followers. Instead He exposed the motives of their hearts and then laid out His requirements for discipleship, in deliberately offensive language.

Jesus answered, "Very truly I tell you, you are looking for me, not because you saw the signs I performed but because you ate the loaves and had your fill. . . .

"Very truly I tell you, unless you eat the flesh of the Son of Man and drink his blood, you have no life in you. Whoever eats my flesh and drinks my blood has eternal life, and I will raise them up at the last day. For my flesh is real food and my blood is real drink. Whoever eats my flesh and drinks my blood remains in me, and I in them. Just as the living Father sent me and I live because of the Father, so the one who feeds on me will live because of me. This is the bread that came down from heaven. Your ancestors ate manna and died, but whoever feeds on this bread will live forever."

—JOHN 6:26, 53–58

As New Testament believers, we know Jesus was not telling them to literally eat His physical flesh and blood. He was talking about the concept of Communion, the symbolic meal in which we celebrate our spiritual fellowship in His sacrificial death and resurrection life. But Jesus didn't explain any of that to them in that moment. He allowed them to wrestle with this hard teaching to expose just how much they trusted Him. A statement I heard from a preacher years ago has always stuck with me: "Jesus was constantly making it easy to leave and hard to stay." In the end, many people decided they couldn't follow Him anymore. Jesus even asked His twelve disciples if this would be the deal breaker in their relationship with Him. But Peter said, "Lord, to whom shall we go? You have the words of eternal life. We have come to believe and to know that you are the Holy One of God" (vv. 68–69).

The disciples were willing to trust Jesus even when they didn't understand Him, because they'd come to believe and know who He really is. If we truly believe that Jesus is King of Kings and Lord of Lords, then He alone is worthy to sit on the throne of our hearts. He is the one we are to trust, follow, and obey above all, and everyone else must be demoted from that position. This is what Jesus was talking about when He told us to count the cost of following Him.

> Now great multitudes went with Him. And He turned and said to them, "If anyone comes to Me and does not hate his father and mother, wife and children, brothers and sisters, yes, and his own life also, he cannot be My disciple. And whoever does not bear his cross and come after Me cannot be My disciple. For which of you, intending to build a tower, does not sit down first and count the cost, whether he has enough to finish it—lest, after he has laid the foundation, and is not able to finish, all who see it begin to mock him, saying, 'This man began to build and was not able to finish'? Or what king, going to make war against another king, does not sit down first and consider whether he is able with ten thousand to meet him who comes against him with twenty thousand? Or else, while the other is still a great way off, he sends a delegation and asks conditions of peace. So likewise, whoever of you does not forsake all that he has cannot be My disciple."
>
> —LUKE 14:25–33 NKJV

In all of His confrontations with people about their trust, Jesus was communicating what it costs to follow Him: everything. We must surrender our entire lives to Him. As Dietrich Bonhoeffer wrote, "One cannot give him only a small compartment in our spiritual life but must give him everything or nothing. The religion of Christ is not a tidbit after one's bread. On the contrary, it is the bread or it is nothing. People should at least understand and concede this if they call themselves a Christian."[2]

One of the sensitive topics I, as a pastor, deal with is what the Bible says regarding our finances. It's something we seem to be guarded about, and many have experienced the abuse or misuse of the teaching on finances. There are many people who struggle when it comes to the principle of the tithe, asking why they should give 10 percent of their income to the church. "Are we still under the law? Is the tithe a New Testament or Old Testament concept?" I don't mind the conversation about finances, and I believe it's healthy to make sure that all we do is founded in Scripture and not just done from a place of religious routine or control. But what concerns me is that this question is usually coming from a deep misunderstanding about the nature of Christianity. While people are wrestling with the concept of the tithe, they are missing the bigger point. People think God is asking them for 10 percent of their money, when God has never asked them for 10 percent of anything. He asks only for all. Let me say that again. God is not asking for 10 percent of your money. He's asking for 100 percent of your money, because He is asking for 100 percent of your life. To choose to follow Jesus is to say, "You can have all of me. That includes my money." That doesn't mean that we must sell everything we own and give it to the poor or the church; it simply means that we freely offer Him all that we have and are from our hearts.

It concerns and saddens me to see believers get thrown off when the journey is harder or more costly than they thought. I've seen many who were passionate about following Jesus, excited about the vision He had placed in their hearts, and committed to the three-mile walk to engage their call. But then they encountered the cost of following Jesus, in a way they didn't expect. They didn't expect it to be that hard or painful or confusing or demanding. It doesn't help that we live in a social media world. I think there are many great things about social media, but one thing it can tend to do is give us a false sense of engagement with no real sacrifice. Not too long ago, if you were engaged in the civil rights movement, it meant you had to travel somewhere and stand on a front line, risking your life. Now we feel like we are fully engaged because we retweeted someone else's statement. The same applies to engaging our call: we don't expect it to cost us, and we seem surprised when it does. But it always has and always will cost us everything to follow Jesus.

Jesus Gives Us All

Jesus doesn't ask us for everything because it's His divine right as our Creator and King, however. He asks for everything because He is inviting us into a covenant relationship, and the nature of that relationship is that both parties give all they are to one another. Jesus asks us to give Him everything because He is offering everything—all He is and has—to us. This is what happened when He invited the one or the few—Moses, the disciples, Evan Roberts, the Brownsville Assembly of God—to partner with Him. When they responded by giving their all, no matter how small or insignificant it seemed, He responded by giving His all. This is how He makes history with us.

This is what we see with the feeding of the five thousand. That miracle began when a boy gave Jesus everything He had—five barley loaves and two small fish. Jesus turned this tiny amount of food into a feast for fifteen thousand. But consider this: couldn't Jesus have performed the same miracle with just one loaf and one fish? Why didn't Jesus take just one of each, multiply them, and let the boy keep the remaining fish and four loaves? He took the boy's whole meal because He requires all. He requires all because He wants to give us all in return and already has given us all on the cross. Responding to His invitation and giving Him all is what allows us to receive the fullness of what He's already given us. It's also how God takes the small, seemingly insignificant offering of our lives and multiplies it to impact the world.

When you say yes to the three-mile walk, you cannot bring a safety net with you. A safety net is something we're trusting in besides God to keep us safe or make us successful. It's part of our lives that we're holding back from Him, saying, "God, I'll give you this much, but please don't take everything." We don't see that withholding from Him is holding back the floodgates of His blessing in our lives. We're holding back the very life we were created for, a life of full engagement and partnership with the one who made us. We're trying to save ourselves, and Jesus told us where that leads: "Whoever wants to save their life will lose it, but whoever loses their life for me will find it" (Matt. 16:25).

When Jonathan and his armor-bearer left on that three-mile walk, they left their safety net behind. They left food and beds and the company and security of the crowd. They had no certainty of success. They did it for one reason: they trusted God and knew that all He needed was a few who were willing to put their lives entirely in His hands. "Perhaps the LORD will act in our behalf. Nothing can hinder the LORD from saving, whether by many or by few" (1 Sam. 14:6). They moved forward and didn't stop until God showed up, and then they kept moving forward.

I want to live that way. I don't want to get to the end of my life and realize I never took risks, never stepped out when there was the possibility it may not work out, never put myself in a spot that required faith for God to show up. Sometimes, when things get hard, scary, and risky, safety sounds appealing. But when I think about how I want to be able to look back on my life, I know it's always better to lean into the risk. That's where I get to show God that I'm truly all in with Him and trusting Him to be all in with me.

Will you do the same? Will you separate yourself from the crowd, leave your fears and your safety net, and respond to the call on your life? Will you be one of the few who raises their hand?

4

—

Set Apart

I grew up in church. Some of my earliest memories are of being in Sunday school classrooms and raising my hand to invite Jesus into my heart. I did that a few times, just to make sure it stuck. I was genuinely saved at four and swam to the pastor in the baptism tank to be baptized when I was five. My family went to church every Sunday without fail, and I sat through a lot of services.

Growing up in church, I heard about the concept of holiness, but it was hard to fully understand. I remember hearing pastors read the verses in which God commands us to be holy like He is holy and thinking, *That can't be what God means. That's impossible. Nobody can be holy like God is holy. He must have meant something else.* So I mainly just skipped over those verses on holiness and didn't think too much about it. But later I discovered that holiness is not something I could skip over or ignore. The journey to engage the call of God on our lives begins with embracing a life of holiness. But how can we embrace a life of holiness when we don't understand what it is, or at best our understanding is faulty or skewed?

Holy means "set apart for God." The pattern we see throughout Scripture is that everyone who answered a call of God first had to separate themselves and be set apart for the call. Jonathan and his armor-bearer had to separate themselves from the Israelite army to fulfill their mission. The same was true of Noah, Abraham, Moses, Jonah, Joshua, David, Esther, the disciples, Paul, and everyone who received a call of God in the Bible. Before He sent them to do something, He separated them. This often involved physical, geographical separation from their families, homes, and normal surroundings, and it always involved a separation of focus, time, and activity. Every person called by God had to be fully set apart to engage that call. Even Jesus was set apart for the call of God on His life. Jesus described Himself as, "[He] whom the Father sanctified and sent into the world" (John 10:36 NKJV). *Sanctify* means to make holy, to set apart. Jesus prayed that we would be sanctified in the same way: "My prayer is not that you take them out of the world but that you protect them from the evil one. They are not of the world, even as I am not of it. Sanctify them by the truth; your word is truth. As you sent me into the world, I have sent them into the world. For them I sanctify myself, that they too may be truly sanctified" (John 17:15–19).

Holiness, being set apart, is essential to our call from God; it is the first thing to which we are called. The Father sanctified Jesus, then sent Him. In the same way, before God sends us to do anything, He first sanctifies us. Charles Spurgeon said, "True and genuine piety is necessary as the first indispensable requisite; whatever 'call' a man may pretend to have, if he has not been called to holiness, he certainly has not been called to the ministry."[3]

Unfortunately, holiness is one of the most misunderstood concepts in the body of Christ. Another reason I ignored holiness while growing up in church, besides thinking it was impossible to be holy as God is holy, was that the way the subject was typically presented turned me off. Whenever God's holiness was discussed, the emphasis was always on His otherness, His separateness from sinful, fallen humanity. It made Him seem cold, distant, and fearful to approach. When it came to the topic of trying to live a holy life, the discussion always centered on the list of rules we should be keeping, the things we should and especially shouldn't be doing. It was legalistic and mostly negative. Neither picture of holiness was attractive or compelling to me.

However, once I started to actively engage the call of God on my life at seventeen, I couldn't get around the clear teaching of the Bible that God is holy and required holiness from everyone He called. "Be holy, because I am holy" (1 Peter 1:16). When I was in my early twenties, a pastor friend of mine gave me a cassette (yes, it was that long ago) of a sermon on holiness from a preacher I had never heard of. I remember listening to the teaching and feeling something come alive inside of me. I was hearing holiness explained in a way I had never heard before. Perhaps there was more to holiness than I understood. It provoked me to dig deeper, and thankfully, I discovered that there was. I discovered that holiness is completely different from what I had learned growing up. This became a foundational moment in my pursuit of God's call on my life.

Holiness is not about God keeping His distance from us or putting demands on us to enter His presence. It's not about our keeping the rules and avoiding certain sins. We are not holy because we don't cuss or watch inappropriate movies or sleep around or listen to bad music. I'm not saying it's okay to do those things; I'm simply saying that not doing those things doesn't make you holy.

I was in full-time youth ministry for twelve years. I can't count the times when sermons ended with a call to the altar to repent of sins. I believe in repentance and believe deeply that it is an important and critical part of the life of a believer. If we are in sin, we need to repent of that sin and separate from it. Holiness absolutely involves separating from sin and pursuing purity in our lives. The problem I began to see was that we called the youth to the altar to repent of their sins, only to see them back there again the next year to repent of the same sins again. I never wanted to downplay those moments, but I couldn't help but feel that we were missing something. Holiness is not just that you leave sin at the altar; it's that you give yourself fully to God. We separate from sin so that we can be set apart unto Him. What makes us holy is being set apart and dedicated fully to God. This is not something scary or negative; it's what we were created for, which means holiness is essential to a thriving, healthy, successful life.

What Does It Mean to Be Set Apart?

A friend of mine used a simple but profound illustration to explain holiness to a group of teenagers. He began to list the various types of brushes you typically find in the home. There's usually a scrub brush kept in the garage, used to clean sidewalks or garage floors. There are bottle brushes by the sink for washing dishes. There are hairbrushes in the bathroom; they may be used individually or shared by family members. And then you have your toothbrush. That toothbrush is solely yours, and it is used for one thing—cleaning your teeth. You don't use it for multiple purposes or share it with multiple people. That would be a violation of its purpose.

It's a simple and silly illustration, but it's a great picture of what holiness is. Your life has one purpose—to be set apart for God, for His glory. Everything He calls us to be and do in this life is part of fulfilling that purpose. Again, that's the reason why we separate from sin—so we can fully give ourselves to God.

The English word holy comes from the same word that means

"whole." Holiness—being set apart for God—is connected to the idea of wholeness—being undivided, clean, intact, and healthy. In the Old Testament, the animals the Israelites offered to God had to be without spot or blemish, as a symbol that whatever we offer to God must be whole. In the same way, we must offer our whole selves to God. He doesn't require perfection; only Jesus was able to offer Himself as a perfect sacrifice to God once and for all. But He does require us to offer all we are. This is the nonnegotiable part of the call to holiness.

A lot of people don't seem to understand this, however. When it comes to setting their lives apart fully for God, they act like they're on an episode of *American Pickers*. If you're not familiar with this show—one of my favorites—it follows Mike Wolfe and Frank Fritz around the country as they comb through old warehouses and barns, looking for valuable antiques. Whenever they find an item they are interested in acquiring, they negotiate with the owner to buy it.

"What would you like to sell this table for?"

The owner will say something like, "I'd like four hundred dollars for it."

"I don't know, four hundred dollars seems a little too much. What about two hundred?"

"I couldn't part with it for that much. You won't find another table like this with the condition it's in. I've had other people interested in it. What about three hundred?"

"I'm not sure I can go that high. What if we split the difference and go with two hundred and fifty?"

Then they shake hands and agree on the negotiated price.

Sadly, this is how many people approach God with their lives. They seem to think it's an option to negotiate how much of their lives they hand over to God. They come to God and He says, "The cost of following Me is your entire life." They say, "Wow, that is more than I thought it would be. I'd like to give You some of my life, God, but I'd also like to keep some of it back." But God says, "It doesn't work like that. I want one hundred percent of your life. I want you to give Me all that you have—the good, the bad, and the ugly. I want your imperfections, your talents, your gifts, your dreams, and your desires. Surrender it all to me." God doesn't negotiate. We can't come to Him and try to figure out what's the lowest cost we can pay to follow Him. Holiness requires us to give all that we are.

Holiness and covenant go hand in hand. Marriage is a powerful picture of what holiness looks like, because marriage is a covenant. On my wedding day, I stood before family and friends and declared covenant vows to SeaJay. I told her that I would be her husband for the rest of my life. I committed to loving her every day, no matter what. But imagine if my vows had included this statement: "SeaJay, I commit myself to you as your husband three hundred and sixty-four days of the year. I'm going to love you and lay my life down for you on every one of those days. All I'm asking is that one day a year, you allow me to be unfaithful to our covenant of marriage." Nobody would take me seriously. We understand that a covenant of marriage means being married 365 days a year—366 on the leap year. Every day, I am married to my wife. Holiness works the same way. Holiness is 100 percent of my life surrendered, given, and committed to God. I'm not saying that if you are unfaithful to God or stumble along the way, you have failed. God looks at the heart. Is your heart set apart to Him? The Bible says we are to "pursue . . . holiness" (Heb. 12:14 NKJV). This means that even when we stumble and fall, our heart must continue to be in pursuit of a life of holiness.

Another reason why holiness is similar to marriage is because it involves crossing a point of no return. It means giving all of you forever. You may have heard the phrase "burning your bridges." We understand that phrase to mean ending relationships, but originally it meant to cut off a means of retreat or escape. It was something armies did when invading a foreign territory. After crossing a bridge, they burned it behind them to eliminate the option of going back. It was a practical sign of their commitment to go forward at all costs, either to be victorious or to perish in the attempt. Holiness means eliminating all of our options to escape or retreat from a life fully surrendered to Jesus and His purpose in the earth.

If you have ever taken a rollercoaster ride, then you have crossed a point of no return. The moment you're buckled in and start to move along the track, you're going to be there for the duration of that ride. There is no deciding you want to get off as you're hanging upside down a hundred feet above the ground. The same is true of cliff jumping, one of my favorite things to do as a teenager. The thrill of cliff jumping comes in that moment when you push off the cliff into the air. After that moment, there's no getting out of that fall; you can't call a timeout halfway down because it was scarier than you thought it would be. You're committed to the fall, and there is no going back.

I remember one cliff jumping trip on which my friends and I brought someone along who had never cliff jumped and wanted to try it. When we got to the creek where the cliffs were, she confidently announced that she was going to jump from a particular spot and began to climb there. Soon she reached the top and came right to the edge of the cliff, with her toes dangling over. "All right, I'm going to jump," she called down to us. "You can do it!" we yelled back at her, watching and waiting. Seconds turned into minutes as she stood there, frozen on the edge. "I don't know what's going on," she groaned. "I just can't jump. I can't move. I don't want to do it." We redoubled our encouragement, urging her to go for it. "All right, all right. I'm going to do it!" she said. But she didn't. She just stood there on that cliff, unable to move. Eventually we just left her alone. She stayed up there for two hours on the edge of the cliff, periodically yelling down to us that she was going to jump but never doing it. Finally, it was time to leave, and since we were her ride home, she climbed down and left with us.

There are a lot of people who say they want to live for God, but when they realize it requires them to cross that point of no return, they freeze. They just can't seem to make that leap of total commitment to a life set apart for Jesus. I believe it's because they don't yet perceive the adventure that God is calling them to. They don't understand that they will never experience the fullness of a life with God while standing on the edge of the cliff. Cliff jumping isn't fun because you stand on the edge of the cliff looking down at the water below. The adventure is in the jump. So many Christians who are saved and going to heaven are living boring, unengaged lives with God because they think Christianity is standing on the edge of a cliff rather than jumping. We will fully set ourselves apart for God, make that jump, only when we understand *why* God requires that of us.

Why Does God Call Us to Be Set Apart?

Exodus tells the dramatic story of how God separated an entire nation for Himself and called them to holiness. After rescuing the children of Israel from Egypt, He brought them to Sinai and announced, "Now if you obey me fully and keep my covenant, then out of all nations you will be my treasured possession. Although the whole earth is mine, you will be for me a kingdom of priests and a holy nation" (Ex. 19:5–6). As the Israelites walked with God and struggled to keep their covenant with Him, He reminded them repeatedly of their call to holiness.

"I am the LORD your God; consecrate yourselves and be holy, because I am holy. . . . I am the LORD, who brought you up out of Egypt to be your God; therefore be holy, because I am holy."

—LEVITICUS 11:44–45

"Be holy because I, the LORD your God, am holy."

—LEVITICUS 19:2

"Consecrate yourselves and be holy, because I am the LORD your God. . . . You are to be holy to me because I, the LORD, am holy, and I have set you apart from the nations to be my own."

—LEVITICUS 20:7, 26

In every case, God's reason for calling His people to holiness is "because I am holy." He was telling them, "I've called you to be like Me."

Why does God want us to be like Him? It's so important that you know the answer to this question. The answer to this question is what motivates us to pursue holiness. His passion for us to be like Him is part of His Father's heart for us. He wants us, His sons and daughters, to imitate Him so we can thrive and experience the fullness of His love. We cannot separate the call to holiness from the heart of God as a Father. When we do that, holiness is no longer the flourishing life God intends it to be but becomes a legalistic duty. Holiness is 100 percent relational.

Parents generally love it when their children look like them. One of the first questions asked parents after their child is born is, "Who do they look like?" The parents then explain what physical characteristics of their child look like those of one or the other parent. From the time our kids were born, my wife and I studied their features to see how and where they resembled us. One day when my first daughter was about a month old, I heard my wife yelling, "Banning! Banning, come here. I want to show you something."

I hurried to the back room of our house, where SeaJay was holding Ellianna. "What's going on?" I asked. "Is everything all right?"

She grabbed our daughter's hand and held up her little finger. "Look at her pinky."

"Okay . . . What am I supposed to be seeing?"

In response, my wife put her pinky next to our daughter's pinky. My wife has a bit of a hitch in her pinky, and Ellianna had the exact same hitch in her pinky. It was evident at a month old. My wife was beaming and couldn't have been prouder. This of course meant that everywhere we went, she showed people how her daughter's pinky looked like her pinky. It brought such great joy to her heart, knowing that her daughter looked like her.

This is what the Father loves too. He wants us to look like Him, not in our external characteristics but in what the Bible calls our inner self—our heart, character, and whole way of being. This has been His plan for people since the beginning. Genesis 1:26 says that God created humankind "in our image, in our likeness." Why? He wants us to partner with Him and represent Him as His delegated authorities in ruling and caring for the earth, and to do that, we must be like Him. And we *are* like Him. We have His DNA, as surely as my daughter has mine and SeaJay's. When God tells us to be like Him, He is not imposing something foreign on us; He is telling us who we really are. We were created to be holy as He is holy.

One key aspect of God's holiness that He created us to imitate is His loving, relational nature. God points to this aspect in

Genesis 1:26 when He refers to Himself in the plural: "Let *us* make mankind in *our* image" (emphasis added). God is Himself a community of persons, a family. Father, Son, and Holy Spirit partner with and represent one another in perfect love, serving each other and working together in complete unity. The holiness of the Trinity is expressed in these loving, whole relationships. God made us like Himself in creating us from these relationships, for these relationships. We were created as an expression of His love, to live in and from His love. Our call to holiness is all about our coming home to our true identity, our true nature, and our relationship with the Father, Son, and Holy Spirit, and living out of that.

Most of us come to God with a distorted view of His character and heart. We see the Father through the broken template given to us by our earthly parents and other authority figures and expect Him to be angry and punishing or distant and cold. We think He is looking for slaves, employees, workers—people who will obey Him without question but also without intimacy.

Jesus revealed a very different picture to us. Jesus is the only person in history who has perfectly fulfilled God's command to be holy as God is holy. He lived a life that was fully surrendered, sanctified, and consecrated to God. He was completely obedient to the Father, to the point of going to the cross. He never did anything to step outside the Father's authority or misrepresent Him. But Jesus was the farthest thing from the Father's employee. Jesus explained that the relationship between the Father and the Son was an intimate partnership driven by love and honor.

"The Father loves the Son and has placed everything in his hands."

—JOHN 3:35

Jesus gave them this answer: "Very truly I tell you, the Son can do nothing by himself; he can do only what he sees his Father doing, because whatever the Father does the Son also does. For the Father loves the Son and shows him all he does. Yes, and he will show him even greater works than these, so that you will be amazed."

—JOHN 5:19–20

Jesus said, "When you have lifted up the Son of Man, then you will know that I am he and that I do nothing on my own but speak just what the Father has taught me. The one who sent me is with me; he has not left me alone, for I always do what pleases him."

—JOHN 8:28–29

"The reason my Father loves me is that I lay down my life— only to take it up again. No one takes it from me, but I lay it down of my own accord. I have authority to lay it down and authority to take it up again. This command I received from my Father."

—JOHN 10:17–18

Everything Jesus did to fulfill His call on the earth flowed from this place of intimacy with the Father. The accounts of Jesus' baptism show that this intimacy was established long before Jesus began His ministry. Before Jesus preached a sermon, performed a miracle, or called His disciples, His Father proclaimed over Him, "This is my Son, whom I love; with him I am well pleased" (Matt. 3:17). The Father's love was not based on Jesus' performance; Jesus' performance was based on the Father's love. This is what He modeled for us.

Holiness is not a call God gives to employees; it's a call He gives to sons and daughters. Ultimately, the reason the Father wants us to be set apart fully for Him is so He can lavish us with His love, not just once but over a lifetime and into eternity. This is why He invites us into an intimate, permanent, family relationship as His sons and daughters. It's in the context of this relationship that He can show us His heart, nature, and character as our Father and invite us to imitate Him as a response to His love. This has been His plan and desire for us from before the creation of the world. "How blessed is God! And what a blessing he is! He's the Father of our Master, Jesus Christ, and takes us to the high places of blessing in him. Long before he laid down earth's foundations, he had us in mind, had settled on us as the focus of his love, *to be made whole and holy by his love.* Long, long ago he decided to adopt us into his family through Jesus Christ. (What pleasure he took in planning this!) He wanted us to enter into the celebration of his lavish gift-giving by the hand of his beloved Son" (Eph. 1:3–6 MSG, emphasis added).

True holiness is always a response to the love of the Father. He asks us to give ourselves fully to Him because He has already given Himself fully to us. It was the Father's love that moved Jesus to set Himself apart to lay down His life for the world, and it's this love that leads us to obey His command to be holy as He is holy. We don't embrace holiness because it's a bunch of nos; we embrace holiness because it's about love, and love is one big yes—our yes to God in response to His yes to us. Whatever we say no to in a life of holiness is simply a consequence of that one big yes. Incidentally, that's how it works in marriage too. When I said yes to SeaJay on our wedding day, that yes was so complete that every decision I have made since then has been filtered through that yes. There are many things I say no to because of that yes, but most of the time I'm not even aware of them. I don't really have to think about saying no to things, because my yes was so strong and has made the decision for me. The same is true when we say yes to being holy as He is holy. When we believe that Christianity is just a bunch of nos, we miss the true joy of following Jesus with our yes.

How Do We Set Ourselves Apart?

Answering our call to holiness begins with receiving the revelation of the Father's love for us. Revelation is different from information. Information is something we know *about*, but revelation is something we *know*. It's knowledge that has become real through experience and thus has the power to transform our life. Somebody can tell us that God loves us, but we need to encounter that love for it to change us and awaken our hearts in a way that moves us to respond to His love. Only encountering the Father's love will lead us to set ourselves apart fully for Him. As I mentioned in chapter 1, the primary purpose of spiritual disciplines in our lives is to position us to become aware of God's presence, hear His voice, and experience His love in a tangible, personal way. The classic disciplines of prayer, worship, praise, reading the Bible, meditation, fellowship with other believers, fasting, and Sabbath are all designed to lead us past knowing about God's love into experiencing it.

The reason why we establish these as regular practices in our lives is because we don't need just one encounter with God's love to lead us into a life of holiness; we need a lifetime of encountering His love. That's what the Christian life, a holy life, was designed to be: an ongoing dance of encountering and responding to God's love. This is what Jesus was calling us to when He instructed us to abide in His love: "As the Father loved Me, I also have loved you; abide in My love" (John 15:9 NKJV). If we're struggling to make that cliff jump into a life of full surrender to Jesus, or if our love and commitment to Him has grown cold, what we need is not to work harder or muscle our way toward holiness. We need a fresh encounter with His love. When Jesus tells those of us who have grown lukewarm in our faith to return to our first love (Rev. 2:4–5), He's not telling us to go back to the way we loved Him when we first got saved. He's telling us to return to abiding in His love and responding to the revelation of His love for us. All Jesus calls us to must be rooted in, and is impossible apart from, His love for us.

Being transformed by the love of God is what the process of sanctification is all about. Sanctification is different from justification. *Justification* is a legal word that means a change in status from guilty to innocent. When we accepted the work of Christ on the cross and asked God to forgive us of our sins, we received justification; our legal status moved from guilty to innocent. You were justified at your conversion. It happened one time, once and for all. God now looks at your life through the blood of Jesus and sees you as innocent. You can never be more justified than you are now. Sanctification, on the other hand, is a process. The term comes from two Latin words—*sanctus*, which means "holy," and *ficare*, which means "to make." Sanctification is the journey of working out our salvation—learning to live out of our restored relationship with God. Working out our salvation does not mean working *for* our salvation. We cannot work for our salvation; Jesus did that work, and it is complete. All we do is receive it. But once we receive it, it must transform us, and this is a process that requires our participation. We must allow God to make us holy—to teach us how to align our thoughts, motives, words, and actions with His.

Theologian Wayne Grudem says, "Sanctification is a progressive work of God and man that makes us more and more free from sin and like Christ in our actual lives."[4] Yes, though we have been justified before God and forgiven of sin through the cross of Jesus, we also need to learn to walk in freedom from sin. Scripture is clear that this freedom comes not through behavior modification but through renewing our minds and hearts. All sin in our lives is rooted in lies we have believed about God and ourselves, which have caused our minds and hearts to become bent toward trying to trust in, protect, love, and save ourselves. When we are born again, we commit to unlearning these habits of the heart and replacing them with a heart that trusts, follows, and loves the Father just like Jesus did. That process involves exposing and confronting everything in us that isn't fully aligned with His heart. David prayed, "Teach me your way, LORD, that I may rely on your faithfulness; give me an undivided heart, that I may fear your name" (Ps. 86:11). The New King James Version says, "Unite my heart." Whenever we find ourselves struggling to surrender fully to Him, we are coming up against a place where our hearts are divided. We must be healed of this division in order to walk in holiness as God intends.

Right after Paul tells us to "work out [our] own salvation with fear and trembling," he says, "for it is God who works in [us] both to will and to do for His good pleasure" (Phil. 2:12–13 NKJV). This is the beauty of our call to holiness. God doesn't call us to be holy as He is holy and then leave us to figure it out on our own. He calls us to holiness and then works in us to bring it about. He births a desire within us to pursue holiness, and then empowers us in the pursuit of holiness. First Thessalonians 5:23–24 says, "May the God of peace Himself sanctify you completely; and may your whole spirit, soul, and body be preserved blameless at the coming of our Lord Jesus Christ. He who calls you is faithful, who also will do it" (NKJV). I love that promise. We don't sanctify ourselves. The one who called us to be sanctified is also the one who sanctifies us.

This is why God gives us His Holy Spirit. His very name points to His role in our lives: He is our Helper in holiness. "The Helper, the Holy Spirit, whom the Father will send in My name, He will teach you all things, and bring to your remembrance all things that I said to you" (John 14:26 NKJV). He is the one who makes the Father's love real to us, "the Spirit of adoption by whom we cry out, 'Abba, Father'" (Rom. 8:15 NKJV). He is the Spirit of truth who leads us into all truth, setting us free from the lies that have held us bound. He is the one who wields the sword of the Spirit—the Word of God—in our lives to discern the thoughts and intents of our hearts and unite them to love God. Our job in the sanctification process is simply surrendering to the work of the Holy Spirit in our lives.

In 2 Corinthians, Paul gives us an important picture for how the Holy Spirit sanctifies and transforms us: "The Lord is the Spirit; and where the Spirit of the Lord is, there is liberty. But we all, with unveiled face, beholding as in a mirror the glory of the Lord, are being transformed into the same image from glory to glory, just as by the Spirit of the Lord" (2 Cor. 3:17–18 NKJV).

In the journey of holiness, the Holy Spirit is first concerned not with changing our behavior but with enabling us to be with Jesus and behold Him, for this is how we become like Him. This is the pattern we see with Jesus and His disciples: He called them first to be with Him, and then He sent them out. "He went up on the mountain and called to Him those He Himself wanted. And they came to Him. Then He appointed twelve, *that they might be with Him* and that He might send them out to preach, and to have power to heal sicknesses and to cast out demons" (Mark 3:13–15 NKJV, emphasis added).

Jesus doesn't first call us to send us. He first calls us to be with Him, for it is by being with Him that we are shaped by Him. This is where He forms our values, imparts His strength, and establishes His priorities in our hearts. And the Holy Spirit is the one who makes Jesus' presence real to us. Jesus told His disciples that it was better that He was going away so that the Holy Spirit could come live inside them (John 16:7). The Holy Spirit enables us to be with Jesus and behold Him in a way that was not available to the people who followed Jesus during His earthly ministry. This is how He helps us become like Jesus.

In 2 Corinthians 4, Paul goes on to say, "Even though our outward man is perishing, yet the inward man is being renewed day by day" (v. 16 NKJV). It is our inner self—our heart and mind—that the Holy Spirit is transforming from glory to glory into the image of Jesus. This is why the fruit that the Spirit produces in our lives isn't a list of behaviors but a set of heart and character dispositions. "The fruit of the Spirit is love, joy, peace, longsuffering, kindness, goodness, faithfulness, gentleness, self-control. Against such there is no law" (Gal. 5:22–23 NKJV). This list is a description of Jesus' character. He is loving. He is kind, good, and faithful. He is the Prince of Peace. When the Holy Spirit produces His fruit in our lives, we look like Jesus. The law cannot renew our inner self or make us like Jesus; only the power of the Holy Spirit can do that.

If the Holy Spirit was given to us to help, it's silly not to ask for help. You may have heard the phrase, "It's not what you know but who you know that matters." I find this particularly true in my life when it comes to anything handy that needs to be done at my house. I am the opposite of handy, so whenever I need something done at the house that requires any level of expertise, I get on the phone and call a friend who has the knowledge, skill set, and tools to do the job. If I had a close friend who not only had all those things but also was constantly telling me they would love to come and help anytime I needed something done, why would I not get on the phone and call them? Why would I not take advantage of the tools and skill set offered freely by my friend? God gave us the gift of the Holy Spirit. Why would we not utilize that gift to walk in holiness and become like Jesus?

The Power of a Life Set Apart

Scripture shows us that every person who sets himself or herself apart for God has an impact on the world, and that everyone who had an impact and did great things with God first set themselves apart for him. Jonathan and his armor-bearer are no exception; they chose to set themselves apart from the group to do what God had put in their hearts, and as a result the entire nation of Israel saw God defeat their enemies and were liberated from fear. Shadrach, Meshach, and Abednego are other great examples. When all others were bowing, these three men stood, even though they knew it would cost them their lives, because they had set themselves apart years before as young men, when they made a commitment that they were not going to partake in the king's delicacies, because they bowed to a higher authority. When they refused to bow to Nebuchadnezzar, it created an opportunity for their King, the Lord, to show up and demonstrate His superior authority for all to see.

Answering the call to holiness, separating ourselves fully unto God, is what gives us the authority and authenticity to show the world that God is real. Without a life of holiness, we may tell people about Jesus, but we won't be able to show them what He is really like. A holy life sends the message that what Jesus did for us was so glorious that it's worth everything we are. This is why genuine holiness is extremely compelling and attractive. C. S. Lewis said, "How little people know who think that holiness is dull. When one meets the real thing . . . it is irresistible. If even 10% of the world's population had it, would not the whole world be converted and happy?"[5]

So don't be afraid to separate from the crowd. You weren't meant to fit into the world; you were meant to change it by living in a different reality, which you can access only by setting yourself fully apart for God.

MILE 2
-
COURAGE

COURAGE IS CONTAGIOUS. WHEN A
BRAVE MAN TAKES A STAND, THE SPINES
OF OTHERS ARE OFTEN STIFFENED.

—Billy Graham

5

It Takes Courage

When I was twenty-five years old and just a few years into youth pastoring, the Lord spoke to my heart, telling me to put on a conference for youth pastors. The idea was way out of my comfort zone, and I began to argue with God. *Why would I do that? I can't teach youth pastors anything. I can't teach anyone how to grow their youth group. I'm trying to figure it out myself. I don't feel like I know what I'm doing in youth ministry.*

During this back-and-forth with God, He made it clear that He wasn't asking me to teach youth pastors how to grow their youth groups. All He wanted me to do was encourage the youth pastors. I thought, *I can do that. I can always bring in other people to train and equip them.*

So I started a yearly gathering for youth pastors, and I was clear with what I was to do: be their biggest encourager. Doing this shifted something for me in my leadership and set me on a path of understanding one of the main mandates God has given me. I want to come alongside people and put courage inside them. I want to be the biggest encourager in every room I enter. I don't always accomplish that goal, but that is who I desire to be. When people encounter my life, I want them to leave with more courage than they had before. When they hear a sermon I preach, sit in my office, come to my house, have a conversation with me in the hallway, I want them to leave full of courage. One of the reasons I wrote this book is to encourage you in your journey.

One of the biggest reasons I'm so passionate about encouragement is that engaging the call of God on our lives requires courage. You will not become who God has called you to become or get where God has called you to go apart from courage. As a leader, it's easy to get excited about a big vision and articulate it to others. But having a vision and engaging a vision are two different things. The minute you start to engage that vision and try to get from point A to point B, you discover that you need courage. Jonathan had a vision that he articulated to his armor-bearer: "Come, let's go over to the outpost of those uncircumcised men. Perhaps the LORD will act in our behalf. Nothing can hinder the LORD from saving, whether by many or by few" (1 Sam. 14:6). But setting out on that three-mile walk was what really called his courage into play. When you get up like Jonathan did and take that three-mile walk to engage your call, you quickly realize that it takes a massive amount of courage. I think Jonathan knew this; this is why he recruited an encourager to go with him! Only when he had his armor-bearer's support did he set off on the journey. I want my life to be spent in helping people find the courage they need on that three-mile valley of engaging their vision.

So often, I find that a lack of courage is the one thing holding people back from moving forward in their call. They have plenty of information, talent, training, skills, and other resources. They simply aren't being brave in stepping forward. As I shared in my first book, *Jesus Culture*, I remember teaching at a training event for students from more than fifty universities and colleges across

America who had gathered to learn how to reach their campuses for Christ. As I was teaching, I could tell that they were hungry for what I was telling them, but I also had a sense that it was not new information for them. They already knew it. *They don't need more teaching or tools*, I realized. *They just need courage to do what God has told them to do. The reason they're not reaching their campuses the way that they want is because they lack courage.* I shifted how I taught. It's not that I stopped teaching; it's imperative that people are taught and equipped. But my goal was no longer just giving them the right information; it was also instilling in them courage.

Realizing Vision Requires Work

The courage we need on the three-mile walk isn't primarily the courage to make grand leaps of faith or take huge risks. It's primarily the courage to keep walking—to keep doing the work required to move from point A to point B. So many people stop in the middle of the three-mile walk and retreat to the hill because they weren't prepared to deal with the work required to make the journey.

When my kids were little, I used to see these fully assembled playground sets at the entrance of Home Depot. They were wooden structures with a two-story fort, swing set, climbing wall, rope wall, and a slide. Every time I passed them, I thought, *Those things are amazing. I so wish I could get one for my kids.* However, I just couldn't afford it.

Then one day, my father-in-law was visiting from out of town, and we had to run down to Home Depot to grab a few small things we needed. As we walked by the playground sets, he turned to me and said, "Banning, I want to get one of those for the grandkids."

I couldn't have been more excited. I forgot all about the other items I was supposed to pick up, and we went straight to the counter to purchase this playground set I had been wanting for so long. We paid for it and scheduled a delivery date, and I walked out a happy man. On the drive home, I could see in my head exactly where I was going to put this playground in our back yard. I could see my kids playing on it with all their neighborhood friends, and how excited they were. I was going to be the hero dad in the neighborhood.

A few days later a flatbed truck drove up and dropped off the playground in my driveway. I rushed outside to see it. My excitement quickly dimmed, however, when I realized that it hadn't come fully assembled. I probably should have known that—it was fairly obvious—but it hadn't even crossed my mind. What I had seen at the store was not what was delivered to my house. What showed up on my driveway was a pile of boxes and stacks of wood. As I mentioned before, I am not that handy, so I was overwhelmed. But I decided to get to work and build the playground. It was much harder and took much longer than I thought it would. It took me four days, and I had to call ten friends to come help me before we finally got it built. Man, was I frustrated in the process.

It's easy to be excited about the picture you see of your call. It's another thing when it shows up in pieces and you have to build it. It's easy to look at the map of your vision and be excited about where point B is. It's another thing to understand that between where you are at point A and point B is a journey, and that journey involves work. Can you be as passionate about the work needed to fulfill the vision as you were when you received the vision? We need courage to do the work, because the work is hard. It will require us to learn things we never knew and develop skills we don't have. It will require us to face our areas of weakness and immaturity and learn from our mistakes. And it will require us to ask for help, endure frustration, and not give up until the work is done. All of that takes courage.

Do We Know How to Position Ourselves for Courage?

We can't fulfill the call of God on our life without courage. We can't be who He is asking us to be, or do what He's asking us to do, without courage. This is why the enemy's primary objective is to discourage us—to strip us of our courage. Satan knows we cannot be and do what God has called us to be and do without courage, so he comes to disarm us of our courage. If he can't intimidate us into not even starting the three-mile walk, then he does all he can to take us out on the journey. It's so important to understand this, because so many people are discouraged because they are facing discouragement, not realizing that discouragement is something we all face.

I meet so many people who are engaged in the call of God on their life and dealing with discouragement. They come from all walks of life, all levels of leadership, all kinds of talent, all family backgrounds, all economic situations, all careers. Many are successful in what they do. Discouragement may not be debilitating them or hitting them in every area of their lives, but it is something they deal with. The problem with discouragement is that when you live discouraged, you no longer lean in and take risks. You no longer want to dream and press into the things that God has called you to do. You give up hope, disengage, and sit down. As someone who is called to be great and do great things for God, you cannot afford to live discouraged. It's too costly. We must understand that the question is not whether we will face discouragement—that is a given—but what we will do when we face it.

Consider what the children of Israel did when they went to battle against their brothers, the Benjaminites, and experienced a discouraging outcome. "The men of Israel went out to battle against Benjamin, and the men of Israel put themselves in battle array to fight against them at Gibeah. Then the children of Benjamin came out of Gibeah, and on that day cut down to the ground twenty-two thousand men of the Israelites. And the people, that is, the men of Israel, encouraged themselves and again formed the battle line at the place where they had put themselves in array on the first day" (Judg. 20:20–22 NKJV).

Twenty-two thousand men died in a battle—brothers, fathers, cousins, nephews, uncles, sons, and grandfathers. It was a discouraging, heartbreaking day for the Israelites. But they refused to stay in that place of discouragement. They encouraged themselves and formed the battle line again. They experienced victory that day, not because they somehow were able to avoid discouragement but because they knew what to do when discouragement came. They encouraged themselves; they found their courage again.

It's discouraging when things don't work out like we thought. When we lose a business or a home, when a marriage fails, when illness strikes, when things are harder than we expected, it can feel like life is crumbling around us. The question is, do we know how to encourage ourselves? Do we know how to form our battle line again? Those who have accomplished great things for God have faced discouragement, but they knew how to reform their battle line. They encouraged themselves, and they went again. How did they do this?

Lies and Truth

Learning to encourage ourselves begins with understanding what brings us either courage or discouragement. It's critical that we, as believers, become wise about how the enemy works to discourage us. According to the apostle Paul, the enemy operates with schemes that we can identify and be aware of "so that no advantage would be taken of us by Satan, for we are not ignorant of his schemes" (2 Cor. 2:11 NASB). Satan has battle plans and certain ways he attacks us, but Paul was confident that believers will not be outsmarted, outwitted, or taken advantage of by the devil when we understand how he works.

Jesus told us very clearly what Satan's job description is, and what His own job description is. "The thief does not come except to steal, and to kill, and to destroy. I have come that they may have life, and that they may have it more abundantly" (John 10:10 NKJV). The thief, Satan, comes to steal, kill, and destroy; that's his job description. And lies are his weapon of choice to do his job. Jesus called him the father of lies. "He was a murderer from the beginning, not holding to the truth, for there is no truth in him. When he lies, he speaks his native language, for he is a liar and the father of lies" (John 8:44). The enemy tells lies to trap people in discouragement and bondage.

In the garden, the enemy told Adam and Eve lies about God and about themselves. When they believed these lies and acted on them, it separated them from God and led them into bondage to the enemy. This is why lies are so destructive. They separate us from God's character, His nature. They separate us from what He thinks about us. They separate us from His love, grace, freedom, and power. Satan is constantly looking for access points in order to plant lies in our lives so he can steal, kill, destroy, and ultimately hinder us from fulfilling the call of God.

Jesus' job description is also clear: He came to give life, and life more abundantly. He came to restore everything the enemy has stolen, killed, and destroyed through deception and bondage. Jesus does this by bringing the truth of who God is and who we are, to free us from every lie of the enemy and reconnect us to God, ourselves, and one another. He promised, "You shall know the truth, and the truth shall make you free" (John 8:32 NKJV). That word *know* is talking about revelation, not information. Encountering the truth of who God is through the person of Jesus—who is the Truth—is what breaks off discouragement and bondage and leads us to courage and freedom.

Elijah and the Three Lies

At the root of all discouragement are lies we're believing because we listened to the enemy. We all battle with lies, even pastors like me, whose job it is to teach the Bible. I still find myself discouraged at times because I've believed a lie about God, myself, my wife, family, finances, or future. The more I have done battle with the lies of the enemy and encountered the truth that sets me free, however, the more I have come to see that the enemy's arsenal is limited. He has a small repertoire of lies that he uses on every one of us because, well, they work. But the more we become wise to his schemes, like Paul said, and recognize these lies when they come at us, the quicker we will seek the truth that restores our courage.

The story of Elijah is one of the most profound studies on the age-old lies we believe that lead us into discouragement. Elijah ended up in a pit of discouragement right after an astounding mountaintop victory. On Mount Carmel, he orchestrated a showdown between the God of Israel and 450 prophets of Baal. God responded to the prayer of Elijah and brought fire down on his altar and consumed the water-soaked sacrifice, turning the hearts of the nation back to Him in a moment. Elijah then rounded up the false prophets and executed them. Finally, he prayed for rain to end the drought that had devastated Israel by causing three and a half years of famine, and the rains came. It's one of the most incredible accounts in Scripture of a human being standing in radical trust and obedience to God, and of God responding in power. But right after Elijah witnessed God showing up like this, he heard that Queen Jezebel had sworn to take his life. The spirit of fear overtook him, and he ran to hide. He ended up alone out in the wilderness, praying for God to kill him. "When he came to Beersheba in Judah, he left his servant there, while he himself went a day's journey into the wilderness. He came to a broom bush, sat down under it and prayed that he might die. 'I have had enough, LORD,' he said. 'Take my life; I am no better than my ancestors'" (1 Kings 19:3–4).

As the Lord interacts with Elijah, we see that Elijah was believing three lies that led him to this place of discouragement, defeat, and despair. We also see that these lies were not elaborate or obscure, but all too familiar. They are the lies that the enemy uses to discourage all of us. "Elijah was a man with a nature like ours" (James 5:17 NKJV), after all, so it shouldn't surprise us that he struggled just as we struggle. Thankfully, his story is in the Bible to help prepare us to face and overcome these lies in our lives.

The first lie Elijah believed was that God had abandoned him. I encounter Christians all the time who are believing this lie. They would never say they don't believe in God, but their actions indicate that they don't really believe He is with them. They have become what I call "situational atheists." Most believers don't turn into full-blown atheists when they get discouraged, but they do become situational atheists. They believe God exists; they just don't believe He's God of their particular situation. They believe He's got the whole world in His hands, as the Sunday school song says, but He isn't holding the circumstances they're facing with their finances, their marriages, their children, or other personal struggles.

Years ago God challenged me never to approach a situation as if He weren't with me. He showed me that in every situation in which I found myself discouraged, a big part of the problem was that I was believing He wasn't there. I was approaching the struggle with my kids or money or SeaJay or work as though He weren't there. When we look at our situation through a lens without God, things look impossible that are possible with Him. Jesus said, "With men this is impossible, but with God all things are possible" (Matt. 19:26 NKJV). Again, the three-mile walk is impossible without God. The people God calls us to be, and the things He calls us to do, work only in the context of intimate partnership with Him. So as we engage our call, the minute we step off and try to go it alone, it's going to look impossible. The moment we stop abiding in God, we open ourselves to discouragement. When we end up in this place, it's essential that we come back to the truth that God is with us. He hasn't abandoned or forsaken us. It may be impossible with men, but we aren't with men; we are with God.

The second lie Elijah believed was that the situation was hopeless. Nothing says, "I feel hopeless" more than lying down under a bush and saying, "God, kill me now." Hopeless people stop moving forward. They believe there is no future, or what future there may be is bad, so they have no reason to continue forward. They sit down, lie down, and wait to die. People with hope, however, keep moving forward.

The truth we must encounter to free us from this lie is that in the Christian life there is no such thing as a hopeless situation. I have often heard my friend Steve Backlund say, "Any thought in our minds that is not sparkling with confident hope indicates that it is under the influence of a lie."[6] The New Testament is filled with verses about the unshakable hope we have in Christ. Paul even calls God the God of hope. "May the God of hope fill you with all joy and peace as you trust in him, so that you may overflow with hope by the power of the Holy Spirit" (Rom. 15:13). The God of hope is with us and lives inside us. His thoughts toward us are full of hope. "I know the thoughts that I think toward you, says the LORD, thoughts of peace and not of evil, to give you a future and a hope" (Jer. 29:11 NKJV). No matter how hopeless a situation may seem, it isn't. Believing this positions us with courage to seek, find, and hold on to hope in every situation.

The third lie Elijah believed was that he was all alone. When God asked him, "What are you doing here, Elijah?" (1 Kings 19:9), he answered, "I have been very zealous for the LORD God Almighty. The Israelites have rejected your covenant, torn down your altars, and put your prophets to death with the sword. I am the only one left, and now they are trying to kill me too" (v. 10). Elijah had become isolated. He believed that nobody else was standing with him on God's side. He was the only one carrying the burden of Israel. Nobody else was pressing in for righteousness. Nobody else was paying the price and sacrificing for the cause of the true King in the nation.

People feel this way all the time. They believe others have abandoned them. They are all alone in their fight. No one else will understand. No one else sees them. They can show up to church every week and sit in the crowd, but they still feel alone. They feel alone in their marriage, and they feel alone with their friends. This lie is dangerous because it keeps them from one of the main sources of encouragement in their lives—community. In their discouragement, they feel justified in not connecting with community, but then that continues the cycle of discouragement.

But they are not alone. You are not alone. Elijah was not alone. God told him the truth: "I reserve seven thousand in Israel—all whose knees have not bowed down to Baal and whose mouths have not kissed him" (1 Kings 19:18). God has provided people in your life to walk with you. That may be hard to see at times, but they are there. God has not left you alone. Sometimes we walk away from the very community God has given us and then complain that we are alone. Even Elijah left his servant behind so he could complain to the Lord about how alone he was. No matter how things look, you are not alone. God is with you, as are other faithful believers.

Becoming Resilient

Please hear me: If you are dealing with discouragement, don't beat yourself up about it. (That only makes it worse.) We all end up discouraged on the three-mile walk. It's not an experience we can avoid; it's an experience we must learn to walk through and become resilient to. The number one way we become the courageous people God has called us to become is by learning to use the tools and resources He has given us to recover from discouragement every time.

In the next chapter, we'll look at some of the tools and resources that help us to stay encouraged and to find our courage again when we fall into discouragement.

6

—

Keep Your Guard Up

The story of Elijah shows us that it's possible to go from moments of great faith and courage to moments of discouragement simply by believing lies. It's probable that as King Saul sat discouraged and powerless under the pomegranate tree, he was believing those same lies (among others)—that God had abandoned him, that his situation was hopeless, and that he was or would soon be alone. But Jonathan, though he was in the same predicament his father was in, didn't listen to lies and fall into discouragement. So how do lies get in, and how do we keep them out?

Lies get in when we drop our guard, and we drop our guard because we get worn down. In the sport of boxing, one of a boxer's most important jobs is keeping their guard up. They keep their hands up to protect their head, because it's the most vulnerable place to be hit. If they drop their guard, then the opponent will have a clear shot at their head, which could end the fight. Defensive boxing strategy is all about keeping your guard up, while offensive strategy is all about wearing your opponent down until they drop their guard and create an opening for a knockout punch.

Elijah had gotten worn down, and it's easy to see why. He was hunted for three and a half years by Ahab and Jezebel for prophesying the drought that ravaged the nation. People were upset with him and blamed them for the famine they were experiencing. It had gotten so bad, he was having to rely on widows, who had very little, to feed him. He then went public with that bold showdown on the mountain, engaged in intense intercession for the rains to come again, and raced King Ahab's chariot on foot to Jezreel (1 Kings 18). It's easy to imagine just how physically, emotionally, and spiritually worn out he had become. Then, in this place of utter exhaustion, he heard that Jezebel had sworn to kill him by the next day. If he hadn't been so exhausted, we can imagine that he would have had the energy to stop and say, "God, You just brought fire down on the mountain, helped me wipe out the false prophets, and sent us rain again. Surely, You can deal with this threat on my life." Instead Jezebel's punch got through Elijah's defenses. He reacted as most of us would and fled for his life, unaware that he was submitting to the spirit of fear and opening himself up for the enemy to lie to him. Truth was no longer a shield that protected him from the arrows of the enemy that were flying at him. He had dropped that shield and become exposed. Psalm 91:4–5 says, "His truth shall be your shield and buckler. You shall not be afraid of the terror by night, nor of the arrow that flies by day" (NKJV). A buckler was a small shield that a soldier fastened to his arm. God's truth protects us and gives us confidence against the lies that come at us in the night and the day. But when we lay down the shield of truth, the arrows that fly at us find a home.

Above All Else

In boxing, it is our heads we must protect, but when it comes to our spiritual battle and protecting our courage, it is our hearts. Again, the Bible makes it very clear that above all else, we're to guard our hearts.

Above all else, guard your heart,
for everything you do flows from it.
—PROVERBS 4:23

Keep vigilant watch over your heart;
that's where life starts.
—PROVERBS 4:23 MSG

When we get discouraged, it's usually because we have gotten worn down and dropped the guard around our hearts, allowing lies to penetrate. It's crazy sometimes how lies that couldn't reach our hearts just days or even hours earlier can get in just because we got tired and dropped our guard. Because the three-mile walk requires huge amounts of courage, guarding our hearts must be our top priority. So many people have been shipwrecked in their faith because they did not prioritize guarding their hearts. It is in those moments when their hearts become exposed and vulnerable and a toxic lie finds a foothold in their lives. Because of lies and discouragement that get in, they end up leaving churches, breaking up their marriages, falling into addictions, and rejecting God, all to their own destruction.

The priority of guarding our hearts reminds me of the egg drop experiment I did in elementary school. Every student had to try to devise a way to drop an egg from a two-story building without breaking it. You could use whatever materials you wanted in order to build a protective structure for your egg—styrofoam, plastic, water, cloth, balloons. It didn't matter how ugly or awkward your structure was; the only thing that mattered was that it kept the egg intact. The sole criteria of success in this experiment was whether the egg was unbroken after you dropped it. If you protected the egg, you succeeded. That's how it is on this three-mile walk: success all depends on keeping our hearts intact.

When we find ourselves under fire in life, when the enemy is coming at us, it's essential that we know how to keep guarding our hearts as the top priority. While I learned this early in my walk with Jesus, it became mission critical for me in what I still consider to be my toughest year in ministry: the year leading up to our planting Jesus Culture Sacramento. Most major organizational transitions tend to test and strain relationships, and this was no exception. I had been on staff at that time for sixteen years at Bethel Church in Redding, California. The leadership there believed deeply in me and had created the environment for Jesus Culture to grow and thrive. Staying connected to community and under the covering of spiritual authority is one of my deepest core values, but there were a few occasions when the tension and conflict became so painful that it would have been all too tempting to allow seeds of bitterness, offense, and unforgiveness to compromise my heart. However, I took each of these moments before the Lord and asked Him to show me how to respond. He enabled me to deal with the hurts and keep my heart guarded and clean of offense. As a result, I not only held on to my core values of community and covering—even when it meant being misunderstood, criticized, or in conflict with the people I'm walking with—but became more passionate about them than ever. When I look back on that year, hard and messy as it was, I know I succeeded because I managed to keep my heart intact.

I see so many believers who are letting their guard down and getting beat up, but instead of stopping to assess what's going on in their hearts and dealing with it before the Lord, they get distracted by things going on around them and end up spending time on things that don't matter. We need to be trained to think and act like combat medics as we take this three-mile walk. Combat medics treat wounded soldiers on the battlefield, using Tactical Combat Casualty Care (TCCC). Phase one of TCCC, called Care Under

Fire, "focuses on a quick assessment, and placing a tourniquet on any major bleed."[7] The first concern of TCCC is "major hemorrhaging and airway complications such as a tension-pneumothorax."[8] When a combat medic reaches an injured soldier on the battlefield, they are looking for two main things: is the soldier losing blood anywhere at a dangerous rate, and can he or she breathe? If they don't understand that these are the top priorities and how to assess the patient's status in these two areas, then they will spend time on things that are not as important. They could end up setting a broken leg when the soldier is bleeding out, or working on a dislocated shoulder when the soldier can't breathe. The trained combat medic knows how to assess quickly what matters most to save lives on the battlefield. Many believers, however, don't know how to assess quickly what matters most when their lives are under fire: "Above all else, guard your heart." When they are discouraged in the battle, their hearts become exposed, creating an opening that allows the enemy to speak lies. When life gets painful and messy, we need to be able to triage the situation and recognize where our hearts are bleeding out and where our spirits are being crushed and deal with that, instead of getting sidetracked by less-critical issues.

Types of Attack

Like a boxer, the enemy has a variety of ways to wear us down and get us to drop our guard. The first one is just an all-out barrage of punches that come at us fast and don't seem to stop. The goal is to overwhelm us with all that is happening. Many times in life, it's just one of those seasons when the statement rings true, "When it rains, it pours." These are what I call the "cat in the U-Haul" seasons.

When my wife, SeaJay, was seventeen years old, she got a cat named Sal. Sal was an indoor cat until she left for college, and then he took to living out in the woods near her parents' house. SeaJay and I started dating in college, and whenever we went home to visit her parents, Sal emerged from the woods to greet her, looking increasingly worse for wear. A few months after we got married, we stopped by to pick up some of SeaJay's furniture. When she saw how matted and skinny Sal was, she couldn't take it any longer. She turned to me and said, "We have to take him home with us." We lived in an apartment that did not allow pets, so we called my parents and asked if they would watch Sal until we got into a home and could keep him. They agreed, and so it was decided: after years of fending for himself in the woods, Sal was coming back with us.

SeaJay and I had rented a U-Haul to bring her things home with us. After everything was loaded, I climbed into the driver's seat of the U-Haul with Sal, and SeaJay got into our car to drive it back. As I took off down the long driveway, Sal stood on my lap with his front paws on the driver's side window, letting out some type of loud cry somewhere between a meow and a screech. *This is going to be a long ride*, I thought, *but I love my wife and this is what she wants.*

Little did I know that Sal's yowling was just beginning. A minute later I felt a rush of warmth on my lap. I looked down to see that, sure enough, Sal had peed all over me. I couldn't believe it. I wasn't even out of the driveway, and already this trip was not going well. SeaJay's granny lived at the bottom of the hill, so I pulled over there and picked up a cardboard cat carrier she had gotten from her vet. It was too small for Sal, but somehow I made it work and got back on the road, wanting to get this three-hour drive home over as quickly as possible. Unfortunately, it was only just beginning. About ten minutes down the freeway, the most disgusting smell I had ever smelled filled the cab of the truck. Sal had had diarrhea inside the box. Whatever he had been surviving on in the woods now filled the truck with stench that was almost unbearable. I drove home with my nose out the window, still drenched in cat urine.

You'll be happy to know that after that harrowing drive, Sal had a wonderful life, though not with us. He went to live with my parents and never left, because my dad fell in love with him and treated him like a prince for the rest of his days. But for me, that unforgettable drive with Sal came to represent those seasons when there is a lot coming at us all at once, so much that we can't even describe it. When we're in a "cat in the U-Haul" season, we get worn down.

Another strategy of the enemy is to hit us in the same place over and over. In boxing, if the opponent is doing a good job at keeping their hands up, the boxer will focus on one area of their body and target it with hits until the opponent finally drops their hands. Perhaps it's in your finances. Things are tight but going okay, and then you get an unexpected bill in the mail. You take some time to find your peace, stand in faith, declare that God is your provider, and go about your day. The next day, your car breaks down. You try not to be overwhelmed and stressed, hoping it won't be anything big, and continue to declare that God is your provider. Then that evening, your kid ends up in the emergency room. You keep getting hit in the same spot again and again, until finally you are worn down and drop your guard.

Last, the enemy will try to wear us down by keeping us in the fight longer than we expected it to last. Have you ever thought a season was over, only to find out it wasn't? That feeling of disappointment and letdown can open the door to discouragement. Many fighters have lost boxing matches because although they were prepared for the earlier rounds, when the fight went longer than they expected, they got tired and dropped their guard. I have seen so many people drop their guard and get hit with discouragement because the fight or season was longer than they expected.

I rarely am away from my family for long periods of time, but a few years ago I spent sixteen days traveling in Australia and Malaysia—the longest stretch I had ever been away from my family since I got married. By the end of that trip, I was so ready to be home. I could feel the relief when, after almost twenty-four hours of travel, I finally landed in Sacramento. All that remained of the trip was the thirty-five-minute drive to my house. I grabbed my luggage, met my ride, and headed home. Finally, I arrived at my house. Just as I was closing the distance to my front door, I looked down and realized that the suitcase I had was not my suitcase. I had picked up the wrong bag at the luggage carousel at the airport. My heart sank. The trip was not over. There was still more. I got back in the car, drove back to the airport, found my luggage, called the lady whose luggage I had picked up, and finally drove back home. Many people drop their guard simply because the season they are in has lasted longer than they thought.

If we want to be successful on this three-mile walk, then we must be able to do two things to deal with the enemy's attacks. First, as in the egg drop experiment, we need to understand that the top priority is to guard our hearts, and we need to do all we can to keep the guard around our hearts up, to stay encouraged. And second, like the combat medic, we need to quickly assess what matters most when we are under fire.

Check under Your House

If we are going to stay encouraged and recover our courage, we must practice heart awareness. So many of us—myself included—were never taught to be aware of what was happening in our hearts. Practicing heart awareness means taking the time to examine our emotions, thoughts, and desires, as well as the beliefs that are driving them. These beliefs are where either lies or truth become rooted in our hearts. However, most of the time we are not aware when these lies start to penetrate at these deep emotional levels. We are reacting to these messages before we have the chance to reflect on whether our internal perceptions, interpretations, and narrative are lined up with the truth. If we ignore what's going on at this foundational level of our heart beliefs, we give these lies the chance to put down roots and erode our courage and faith.

We recently bought a house from a couple who had been its sole owners for twenty-six years. They loved the house, had taken great care of it, and had many fond memories of raising their kids there. We were blessed and excited to be able to buy it from them. As with any house purchase, the bank sent an inspector out to look over every aspect of the house before giving us a loan. The house sits on a hill, and half of its foundation was a concrete slab and the other half raised wood. When the inspector looked at the foundation, he discovered that the entire wooden structure was rotted. He was surprised that half of the house was still standing. In twenty-six years of living there, the previous owners had never checked under their house. The entire foundation on one side of the house had to be replaced.

So many of us don't even know what we are believing, because we don't stop and pay attention to what is going on inside us. Perhaps you were raised like I was. My parents did the best they could with what they were given in their upbringing, but our home was not an emotionally connected home. No one taught me how to recognize what was going on inside me and fueling my decisions and thoughts. When I got married, SeaJay naturally wanted to know what I was thinking, feeling, and wanting. For a long time, I had no idea what to tell her. It wasn't that I was holding anything back; it was that I genuinely didn't know what was going on inside me. I would jokingly tell her, "I'll let you know what is going on inside me when I know what is going on inside me." Practicing internal awareness is something I have had to learn to do as an adult and am continually learning to do better. In the process, I've had to overcome a lifelong habit of neglecting my internal world for too long when things got stressful or discouraging. There were lies impacting my life that I didn't even realize were there.

Danny Silk, who has been a mentor in my life in this area of building internal awareness, once asked me, "When someone sprains their ankle in a game, what do they do?"

"You tape it up," I replied.

Danny shook his head. I threw out a few other answers, but none of them hit the target. He finally told me what he was looking for. "You take yourself out of the game and assess the situation."

This idea seemed so simple and yet foreign to me. I grew up with the belief that if you got hurt in a game, you played through it. You sucked it up, taped it up, got a shot to numb the pain, and pressed on. I was recently at one of my thirteen-year-old son's basketball games, sitting in the stands with the other dads watching the game. In the middle of a play, one of the players on our team fell to the ground in pain, holding his ankle. All the moms were worried he was okay, but his dad, sitting next to me with his arms crossed, just yelled with a tinge of annoyance in his voice, "Get up!" His son ended up being fine. I was laughing because I understood completely. I want my son, as an athlete, to learn how to play through pain, not quit because of some discomfort. But Danny showed me that this approach, which isn't exactly healthy in sports, really gets problematic in our emotional and spiritual lives. When I am hurt, scared, overwhelmed, or feel powerless, it's unhealthy to try to compartmentalize, ignore it, or medicate it and try to move on. I need to stop what I'm doing and take a time-out to assess what's really going on under my house.

As I shared in chapter 1, one of the most difficult years of my life preceded Jesus Culture's New York and Los Angeles arena gatherings in 2012, which, again, were successful in every way except financially. It wasn't just the loss of finances that was difficult; it was also the tension and conflict we had to navigate in relationships within our team. We took a break from arena gatherings while we planted our church, Jesus Culture Sacramento, but a couple of years after we launched, I started to feel a stirring to host conferences in arenas again. I even toured an arena on the East Coast, where we were praying about holding an event. But every time I thought about it, I felt stressed. In the past, I had blown right past stressful feelings like that until they became too obvious to ignore. This time, since I was trying to get better at checking under my house, I slowed down to figure out what was going on inside me. I took some time to take stock of my thoughts and feelings and realized that I was stressed not about putting on the event but about the year leading up to it. I just didn't know if I could handle walking through it again, when my last experiences had been so intensely stressful.

I was in England when I had this realization, and that evening I went to dinner with some pastor friends there. I began to share with them what I was processing (another thing I never used to do), and one of them responded by sharing a story from an article he had just read. The article was about soccer players (or football players, to be true to England) whose careers ended early, not because they weren't physically able to play anymore but because they could not get over an injury mentally. Perhaps they blew out a knee by planting on it wrong in a game. They recovered completely, but when they got back on the playing field, they did not want to fully plant on the knee like they did before, for fear that it would blow out again. So even though they were healthy, they had to retire.

As he shared that story, I realized, *That's exactly what is happening to me. I am scared of blowing out my knee again.* I didn't believe that I had a new set of legs. I didn't believe that God would be there for me if I took that risk again.

This conversation prompted me to take some time to check under my house. In prayer, I invited the Holy Spirit to show me the lies I was believing and replace them with His truth. Once I had aligned my heart with the truth, I regained the courage I needed to move forward again and not stop dreaming or engaging what God had called me to.

If we want to stay encouraged and keep our guard up, we need to make it a regular habit to check under our house, even when things seem okay. Like David, we must invite the Holy Spirit to shine His light on what is going on in our hearts. "Search me, God, and know my heart; test me and know my anxious thoughts. See if there is any offensive way in me, and lead me in the way everlasting" (Ps. 139:23–24). The enemy tries to distract us from practicing awareness like this, because he knows that the minute we bring his lies into the light, we will see them for what they are and reject them. Satan operates in the shadows, in the dark, because that's where his lies have power; he can distort reality and seem bigger and more powerful and intimidating to us when the lights are out. Slowing down to investigate our hearts with the Holy Spirit is how we bring things into the light of truth. As we do that, there are three keys that will help us keep our guard up and keep our hearts healthy.

Key 1: The Power of a Meal and a Nap

Don't underestimate the power of a meal and a nap. Sometimes when we get worn down, the first thing we need to do is recover physically. This was the first thing God did for Elijah when He met him in his place of discouragement. Before He spoke with Elijah and encouraged him with truth, He had him eat a meal, take a nap, and then eat *another* meal (1 Kings 19:5–7). It's easy to forget that the spiritual, emotional, and physical dimensions of our lives are intricately connected. Sometimes we're just worn out physically, and the most spiritual thing we can do is take a nap and eat a meal.

Incidentally, right after Jonathan's mission with his armor-bearer, and the Philistine's spectacular defeat, King Saul makes his men swear an oath that they won't eat anything until they have fully routed the enemy. Jonathan misses the memo and eats some honey. When his men tell him that they're all fainting away because his father's curse will fall on them if they eat, he retorts, "My father has made trouble for the country. See how my eyes brightened when I tasted a little of this honey. How much better it would have been if the men had eaten today some of the plunder they took from their enemies. Would not the slaughter of the Philistines have been even greater?" (1 Sam. 14:29–30). I think Jonathan appreciated the power of a meal not only to restore physical strength but also to "brighten our eyes"—to put fresh courage in our hearts. Jonathan knew what it took to keep his guard up.

When our kids were younger, I often came home from work to find SeaJay waiting near the front door, looking spent. She would say, "Here are the kids. I am going out right now. I will be back later." After the first few times she did this, I made some remark about how I had worked hard all day too.

She looked at me with raised eyebrows and asked, "I'm sorry, did you go to the bathroom by yourself today?"

"Yes, a few times."

"Well, I didn't. So I'm going out and will be back later."

After that I let her go without comment, especially since I saw that the time away helped her recharge. More often than not, she ended up at her favorite store, Target. She would buy a hot pretzel from their food court and aimlessly walk around the store, looking at things while she ate the pretzel. Sometimes she wouldn't even buy anything. People from our church would run into her at Target, just walking around with a pretzel. That was her meal and a nap.

We all need our own meal and a nap, something that restores and refreshes us physically. Sometimes when we are struggling with discouragement, we think we need to go on a forty-day water fast and start getting up at five every morning to pray and press in harder. We think the solution is to stop eating and sleep less. I believe in fasting, and I am deeply committed to prayer. Yes, we need to find refreshing in His presence. Yes, we need to hear from Him. But your spiritual world is connected to your physical world, and sometimes the first thing we need to do is eat and sleep. Go on vacation, watch a movie, get some rest, and eat a good meal.

To stay encouraged and keep our guard up, we must take care of ourselves physically. Establishing habits of good nutrition, regular exercise, and sound sleep may not sound spiritual to us, but they are critical to staying not only energized but encouraged.

Key 2: Keep One Foot in the Water

The second way to keep your guard up and stay encouraged is to practice the presence of God. And if you have become discouraged and are battling lies, your immediate response must be to retreat to His presence.

I met the son of a Vietnam era Navy SEAL who told me that his dad and other SEALs had a phrase: "Always keep one foot in water." Among all soldiers in our Special Forces, SEALs are unique in their ability to thrive in water. In *America's Special Forces*, David

Bohrer writes, "The acronym SEAL identifies the environments in which they operate, sea, air, land. SEALs are first and foremost warriors who come from the sea and return to its silent darkness when their work is done. This distinction alone sets them apart from all other special operation forces—that one of nature's harshest environments, the water, is a safe haven for SEALs. It is where they are most comfortable and confident."[9]

No matter what enemy they're facing, SEALs are confident that if they get into water, the enemy can't follow them there. A SEAL always knows where water is, because if they are in trouble, retreating to water will give them the advantage. He will be comfortable and confident while his enemy struggles against one of nature's harshest environments. The water is where he thrives and where his enemy dies. This is why at all times SEALs keep one foot in the water.

Elijah encountered the presence of God. The presence of God is to us, as believers, like water to a Navy SEAL. For us, the presence of God is where we thrive and where the lies of the enemy die. We're called to always keep one foot in the presence of God, because the moment we retreat to His presence, the lies of discouragement, hopelessness, and powerlessness fall away. The lie that God is not with us dies in His presence. The lie that the situation is hopeless dies there too. And the lie that we're all alone will not survive in His presence. In God's presence, we are filled with the truth that He is with us, that there is boundless hope for our situation, and that we are not alone. This is why being in His presence fills us with courage. The Bible says, "In Your presence is fullness of joy" (Ps. 16:11 NKJV) and "The joy of the LORD is your strength" (Neh. 8:10 NKJV). It also says, "Wait on the LORD; be of good courage" (Ps. 27:14 NKJV).

When we're worn down and discouraged, it's time to retreat to

His presence to have our strength and courage restored. And here's the good news: we can access the presence of God wherever we are. God is no longer confined to a box behind a veil. We don't have to be in a worship service at church to experience His presence. He resides within us and is available to us at all times; all we have to do is turn our attention and affection to Him. We can do that in our car, in a cubicle, as we wake up in the morning, or on a park bench during our lunch hour. It is simply a matter of changing our focus, becoming aware of Him, and allowing His reality, His voice, and His truth to permeate our hearts and perspective.

Key 3: Who You Show Up with Matters

The third thing we need to do to keep our guard up and stay encouraged is not to fight the battle alone. Elijah believed he was all alone, the last boxer in Israel duking it out with the evil Queen Jezebel. But this was a lie; he was fighting alone when he didn't have to. When God met with Elijah, He not only told him about the seven thousand faithful in Israel but sent him to anoint Jehu— the champion who would take on Jezebel—as king of Israel and to anoint Elisha as his apprentice, companion, and successor. God sent Elijah back from the wilderness encouraged, knowing he had partners in battle.

This is the pattern we see throughout Scripture. Whenever God calls somebody, He places somebody beside them as an encourager. Moses encouraged Joshua to prepare him to step into his call to lead Israel into the promised land, as God had instructed: "But command Joshua, and encourage him and strengthen him" (Deut. 3:28 NKJV). Jonathan had his armor-bearer, who put courage in Jonathan when he said, "Do all that is in your heart. Go then; here I am with you, according to your heart" (1 Sam. 14:7 NKJV).

Jonathan later encouraged David to engage his call to be king of Israel. Mordecai encouraged Esther to step into her call with the famous words, "If you remain silent at this time, relief and deliverance for the Jews will arise from another place, but you and your father's family will perish. And who knows but that you have come to your royal position for such a time as this?" (Est. 4:14). In the New Testament, we see Barnabas encouraging Paul, and Paul encouraging Timothy. That is how God works in our lives. He doesn't leave us alone. He puts an encourager or a community of encouragers around us or makes them available to us. If you feel alone in your calling, like Elijah, it doesn't have to stay that way. Ask Him to lead you to encouragers or show you the people He has already put around you to encourage you.

The story of Esther and Mordecai is especially fascinating because it shows us that Esther didn't have the courage to do what God had called her to do apart from the encouragement of Mordecai. It was obvious that Esther had a call on her life. She had favor with the king and was promoted to the position of queen for a reason. But when Mordecai told her to stand before the king and plead for her people—the very thing God had placed her in that position to do—her first response was essentially, "If I go stand before the king, I can die" (see Est. 4:11). Her first reaction was not one of courage and boldness. Only after Mordecai encouraged her was Esther emboldened to risk her life for her calling. "I will go to the king, even though it is against the law. And if I perish, I perish" (Est. 4:16). On her own, Esther didn't have the courage needed to do what God had called her to do. The fulfillment of Esther's call did not happen apart from Mordecai's encouragement.

When we distance ourselves from people and believe the lie that we are all alone, we are separating ourselves from the very encouragement God is trying to release to us so we can become who He has called us to become and do what He has called us to do. There is a courage found only in community—in being surrounded with people who believe in you and challenge you. God puts people in your life to run with you. This is one of His primary resources for helping you keep your guard up and stay encouraged.

I remember my father telling me the story of the day he ran the San Francisco Marathon. San Francisco is usually temperate and cool, even in the summer, but the day of the marathon, a brutal heat wave hit. People were hiding under cars, just trying to get in the shade, and some were passing out with heatstroke. My father managed to finish the race, but it wasn't easy. The organizers of the marathon had placed volunteers all along the route whose sole job was to run alongside the runners and just encourage them. They said, "You're doing a great job. You've started at a great pace. This is what you've prepared for." As the race progressed, they said, "You're over halfway there now. You're on the downhill slope. You can do this." Closer to the end, they said, "You're almost there. I know it's not easy, but you can do this. This is what you have trained for. Don't give up now." The organizers of the marathon were doing everything they could to help the runners succeed. They wanted the runners to keep their spirits and courage up, even in the terrible heat.

I need encouragers like that in my life, and I want to be an encourager in the lives of others. We are meant to be running alongside others, both receiving courage and giving courage. Paul wrote to the church at Rome about how he longed to be with them so they could be encouraged together as he ministered to them. "I long to see you, that I may impart to you some spiritual gift, so that you may be established—that is, that I may be encouraged together with you by the mutual faith both of you and me" (Rom. 1:11–12 NKJV). Every one of us must have people we're encouraging and people encouraging us in our lives. Have you positioned your life in such a way that when you need it, you know how to find courage and courage knows how to find you?

The enemy knows that community is one of our greatest sources of courage; this is why he tries to isolate us from each other. When we allow offense to take root in our lives or bitterness to linger, it separates us from others. As I mentioned before, you cannot afford to be isolated. It is too costly. A big part of keeping our guard up is staying in community, even when we want to run away. So often when I have gotten worn out, dropped my guard, started to believe lies, and ended up discouraged, it has been the community around me who has spoken truth to me and restored my courage. The more I have benefitted from the strength of community in my life, the more ridiculous it seems to me to try to face battles alone. Why would I show up to the battle alone when I don't have to?

I once got a call from a friend who was a worship leader at a church in Colorado Springs. He was putting together a worship leaders vs. preachers basketball tournament after one of the night services at their summer youth conference, where I would be speaking, and asked if I wanted to play.

"Of course!" I told him. "I'm in."

The night of the tournament, we finished a great time of going after God with thousands of young people and headed over to their gym. Unfortunately, as great as the service had been that night, the basketball tournament did not go my way. The preachers team got crushed. We lost almost every game, and I went home demoralized. At the top of my StrengthsFinder test results is competition, so as much as I love playing basketball, I hate losing more. Even though it was a blast playing pickup ball with friends, I went home not very happy.

A couple of months later I got an invitation to speak at the same youth conference the following year, and shortly after that I got another text inviting me to play in the second annual worship leaders vs. preachers basketball tournament. I was relieved to have a chance to redeem myself and make right the debacle of the previous year. After I responded to the invitation, I quickly called Brandon Smith. Brandon is a longtime friend of mine and one of my favorite people to be around. He also happens to be really good at basketball. Brandon was a former point guard for UC Berkeley in the Pac-12 Conference and played professionally internationally. For some time, we had talked about going on a ministry trip together, and I thought this would be perfect. I invited him to go with me on a "ministry trip" that summer, and he said he was glad to come.

I showed up at the conference that year with a new level of confidence. I'm not even sure what I preached about that night. I just wanted to get to the gym. The rematch game was a different story; the preachers ran the floor that night. I'm not even sure if I took a shot, but it didn't matter. I passed the ball to Brandon the entire night and let him go to work.

Who you show up with matters! I may get beaten once, but why would I show up again by myself when I have friends, especially friends who are really good at winning? I don't need to come to the fight on my own and get beaten again.

So many people I know are struggling in areas of their lives but continue to show up to the fight alone. Why would they show up on their own when they are surrounded by community? This is why they're getting beat up and discouraged. We don't have to engage the call of God on our lives alone. We can't do it alone. We must not do it alone.

Jonathan and his armor-bearer made it through that three-mile walk with their courage intact, ready to face their enemies and trust God to make them victorious. They were more courageous at the end of the journey than they were setting out! This overcoming courage is available to us too. We just need to learn to keep our guard up and to quickly take ourselves out of the game to assess the hits to our hearts when they manage to get through. We must become masters in the art of staying encouraged. This journey takes a massive amount of courage, so position your life to stay encouraged.

7

CHAPTER

—

Seasons of Delay

When I was growing up in California, New York City was the city I always looked forward to visiting. I wanted to experience all of the things I had seen so many times in the movies. I wanted to stand on top of the Empire State Building, walk in Central Park, and find a place where I could sit and look at the city skyline lit up at night.

The first time my wife and I were finally able to visit New York City, Ellianna was three years old and SeaJay was seven months pregnant with our second child, Raya. We were excited to explore the city and gather with thousands of others in a stadium to pray for revival in America. On our way there, during our layover in Houston, our plane was delayed. We boarded the plane and lined up on the runway to take off, only to sit on the tarmac for more than an hour before learning that the flight had been canceled and we were heading back to the gate. Once off the plane, we collected our gear (if you have ever traveled with children, you know how many items you travel with—extra luggage, diaper bags, car seats, strollers) and managed to get booked on another flight that would get us into the New York City area later that night. At 11:00 p.m., we landed in New Jersey with no clue how to get to our hotel. This was before smartphones had maps that show you exactly where you are and how to get to your destination. We grabbed all of our luggage and gear and set off to find our hotel. I felt sure it couldn't be that difficult to locate, but that feeling turned out to be wrong. After taking a bus, then a train, and finally the subway, we emerged from underground onto the streets of Midtown Manhattan at 2:00 a.m. Unfortunately, our hotel was not in Manhattan; it was in Queens. I will never forget walking around the city with my seven-months-pregnant wife and two friends, dragging too much luggage and pushing a stroller with my three-year-old daughter, completely lost. We finally made it to our hotel at 5:00 a.m.

I hate delays. I do everything I can to avoid them. I stay away from certain streets, airports, and the freeway during high-traffic hours because I hate delays. I don't think I'm alone in this; so much of the technology of our modern world is built around eliminating delays wherever we find them. From our perspective, things that slow us down and waste our time seem to have no real purpose but to hassle us and cause headaches.

But we have a problem, because God does not hate delays. He uses them frequently on our journey. The three-mile walk to which He calls us is full of delays, and there is no app to help us avoid them. A delay is a gap between the moment when God awakens dreams, speaks promises, calls you to an assignment, or hears your prayers and the moment when those things become reality. Every time we set out to engage what God has called us to be and to do, delay is part of the journey, for a reason. The way we respond to delay plays a critical role in shaping success or failure on this journey.

High Stakes

The Bible gives us many examples of the different ways people respond to delay. Some people did not respond well, and the results are pretty sobering. Consider the story of Aaron and the golden calf.

> When the people saw that Moses delayed coming down from the mountain, the people gathered together to Aaron, and said to him, "Come, make us gods that shall go before us; for as for this Moses, the man who brought us up out of the land of Egypt, we do not know what has become of him."
>
> And Aaron said to them, "Break off the golden earrings which are in the ears of your wives, your sons, and your daughters, and bring them to me." So all the people broke off the golden earrings which were in their ears, and brought them to Aaron. And he received the gold from their hand, and he fashioned it with an engraving tool, and made a molded calf.
>
> Then they said, "This is your god, O Israel, that brought you out of the land of Egypt!"
>
> So when Aaron saw it, he built an altar before it. And Aaron made a proclamation and said, "Tomorrow is a feast to the LORD."
>
> **—EXODUS 32:1–5 NKJV**

In the delay, Aaron led the children of Israel into idolatry. If Moses hadn't been there to intercede, they wouldn't have lived to see another day. Though Moses managed to help them clean up that particular mess with God, their motives for mishandling the delay remained unchanged. They continued to complain and rebel until God declared that they were disqualified from entering the promised land. That generation never fulfilled their call; they died in the desert.

Then there's the story of Saul making sacrifices without Samuel. He did this after learning that the Philistines had amassed their army of six thousand charioteers and uncountable soldiers. With his soldiers trembling with fear, Saul managed to hold them together with Samuel's promise that he would come in seven days to make the required sacrifices to bless the army and inquire of the Lord as to what their strategy should be. When the seven days passed and Samuel didn't come, however, Saul's men began to scatter. In this delay, Saul became desperate, took matters into his own hands, and made the sacrifices. No sooner had he finished the job than Samuel arrived to tell Saul the serious consequences of his presumption. "Samuel said to Saul, 'You have done foolishly. You have not kept the commandment of the LORD your God, which He commanded you. For now the LORD would have established your kingdom over Israel forever. But now your kingdom shall not continue. The LORD has sought for Himself a man after His own heart, and the LORD has commanded him to be commander over His people, because you have not kept what the LORD commanded you'" (1 Sam. 13:13–14 NKJV).

In the delay, Saul fell into disobedience, and the cost was severe: he lost his royal dynasty. The calling of every king was to establish their reign and a royal lineage. By mishandling the delay, Saul disqualified himself from fulfilling that call.

In contrast to Bible stories like Aaron's and Saul's are stories like David's. The man after God's own heart experienced a thirteen-year delay between being anointed king and ascending to the throne. During that time, David had many opportunities to take his call and destiny into his own hands, but every time he refused. As a result, God established his royal dynasty eternally, even choosing to bring His own Son to earth through David's line.

These stories show us that there are high stakes connected

to how we handle delays. In the cases of Aaron, Saul, and David, these stakes were extreme, as they were all leaders whose decisions affected millions of people. But the test in all three situations was the same. Aaron and Saul found themselves surrounded by terrified people pressuring them to act, and they caved to the fear of man. David likewise was pressured by his men to take Saul's life when he had the chance, but he feared God more than man and didn't give in. No matter who we are, this is the test we will face in the delay: either to take matters into our own hands and try to make our call happen according to our strength, our way, and our timing or to stay in a place of trust and surrender and allow God to lead us in His plan for fulfilling our call.

In the delay, we see what's in our hearts. Do we fear man or God? Will we trust ourselves or God? Do we have to be in control, or do we want God to be in control? Only in the delay do these things rise to the surface so we can deal with them and make powerful choices to align our hearts with God's heart for us.

Lazarus and Divine Delay

One of the most powerful biblical examples of a divine delay is the story of Jesus raising Lazarus from the dead.

Lazarus and his sisters, Mary and Martha, were some of Jesus' closest friends and disciples. They had seen Jesus heal and do amazing miracles. When Lazarus became ill, Mary and Martha sent word to Jesus, fully believing that He would come and heal their brother without delay. John's account emphasizes that Jesus loved these people. "Now a man named Lazarus was sick. He was from Bethany, the village of Mary and her sister Martha. . . . So the sisters sent word to Jesus, 'Lord, the one you love is sick.' When he heard this, Jesus said, 'This sickness will not end in death. No, it is for God's glory so that God's Son may be glorified through it.' Now Jesus loved Martha and her sister and Lazarus" (John 11:1, 3–5).

What Jesus did next, however, made no sense to anyone. "So when he heard that Lazarus was sick, he stayed where he was two more days" (John 11:6). During that delay, Lazarus died. It is clear that Jesus intentionally delayed two days. Sometimes we think that every season of delay in our lives is an attack of the enemy, not realizing that Jesus may be involved in the delay. By the time Jesus arrived in Bethany, Lazarus had already been in the tomb for four days. Everyone was confused. His disciples wondered if this was the end of the road for Jesus and they would all soon be dying too (John 11:16). Martha and Mary each ran out to meet Jesus, saying, "Lord, if You had been here, my brother would not have died" (John 11:21, 32 NKJV). And the onlookers at the tomb were asking, "Could not he who opened the eyes of the blind man have kept this man from dying?" (John 11:37).

You can practically hear the thoughts and questions behind these responses. *We thought we knew You, Jesus. We thought You cared. We thought You were all-powerful. We thought You would have the same urgency to fix this problem and want the same outcome. But Your delay is making us question all that. What You let happen in the delay is making us wonder: Do You care? Are You powerful? Why would You let this happen?*

When God does not seem to share our urgency about a situation, we so quickly start to question His character. I've encountered this in my kids. When they are ready and want to leave for school in the morning and I am not in the car yet, they get frustrated. If my urgency to get them out the door on time does not seem to match theirs, my kids react as if I don't care about them. What they are experiencing as a lack of urgency and delay on my part is my seasoned knowledge of exactly how much time I need to take them to school and my lack of worry that anything will happen to make us late. Seasons of delay expose just how easily we move to doubting God because His timing is not our timing. In a delay, truths that seemed so unshakable to us suddenly seem questionable. Is God really good? Does He care? Can't He fix this? Why is He letting this happen?

John's account shows us how Jesus answers the unspoken *Don't You care?* and *Are You powerful?* questions. First, we see that Jesus is anything but cold, disconnected, or unaffected by the prayers of those He loves. John tells us that Jesus was "deeply moved" and wept as He witnessed the mourners at the tomb of Lazarus (John 11:33, 35, 38). He cared, much more than anyone present could possibly comprehend. And when He called Lazarus from the tomb, they all saw that He was far more powerful than they had imagined. His heart of love for them, and His ability to fix the problem, became obvious and undeniable. I need you to hear this. You may be in the midst of a season of delay, and you believe God doesn't care about you or your situation. Nothing could be farther from the truth. God sees you and cares deeply about the things that are in your heart.

Then there was the unspoken question, *Why?* This is a question we will all ask in delays. We think we need an explanation, a reason for what is happening. And Jesus repeatedly answers this question.

> He told [his disciples] plainly, "Lazarus is dead, and for your sake I am glad I was not there, so *that you may believe*. But let us go to him."
>
> —JOHN 11:14–15 (EMPHASIS ADDED)

> Jesus said to her, "Your brother will rise again."
> Martha answered, "I know he will rise again in the resurrection at the last day."

Jesus said to her, "I am the resurrection and the life. *The one who believes in me will live, even though they die; and whoever lives by believing in me will never die. Do you believe this?*"

"Yes, Lord," she replied, "I believe that you are the Messiah, the Son of God, who is to come into the world."

—JOHN 11:23-27 (EMPHASIS ADDED)

Jesus said, "Did I not tell you that if you believe, you will see the glory of God?"

So they took away the stone. Then Jesus looked up and said, "Father, I thank you that you have heard me. I knew that you always hear me, but I said this for the benefit of the people standing here, *that they may believe that you sent me.*"

—JOHN 11:40-42 (EMPHASIS ADDED)

This was the why of Jesus' delay: "that they may believe." Jesus was trying to get them to a place of greater faith. When someone they loved was sick unto death, would they still believe in Jesus, the Healer, the one who not only heals but raises the dead? It's the same why He gives to us in our delays. When things are taking longer or not turning out the way we thought they would, Jesus' answer to our *Why?* is *Trust me.* In the delay, Jesus is after our trust.

Unlearning Mistrust

We often see seasons of delay as a frustration we must endure, instead of recognizing them for what they are—a gift from God to restore us to a place of trust. God designed us to live out of trust in Him. We were created for intimate relationship with Him, and trust is the foundation of every healthy relationship. This is why we are at our freest, healthiest, and most secure when we are living out of deep, abiding trust in God. However, since the fall, our ability to trust God has been damaged and stunted. The fall of humanity was a fall from trust. Adam and Eve mistrusted God's character when they listened to the enemy's lies and then stepped out to take control of their destiny and do things their way. Ever since, humans have been locked in cycles of bondage to mistrust in God and addiction to being in control.

Our need for control is so deeply ingrained in us that we hardly notice it. It's just the way we live. People come over to my house and see me vacuuming and doing the dishes and give me compliments for being helpful. They are impressed that I am serving my family by doing the dishes. While I do have a genuine desire to serve my family, I also have a strong need and desire to do certain things my way. I don't trust anybody else to load and unload the dishwasher. There is a certain way to do it, and for some reason my family cannot seem to figure it out. No matter how many times I try to show them the correct way to load the dishwasher, they are either unable or unwilling to do it the right way! So I just don't trust anybody else to do it, and I do it myself. It looks impressive on the outside, but what's motivating my actions is a lack of trust and a need for control.

When we travel, I don't need a detailed plan, but SeaJay wants to know everything—where we're going, when we're getting there, where we're staying, and what we're doing. I tell her it will be fine and it'll work out, but that never seems to help, and she still wants details. She also always leaves a plan behind for whoever is taking care of our house or watching our kids. I've learned that the bigger her list, the less she trusts the person. When she trusts them more, the list is smaller and less detailed. When she doesn't trust, she tries to control every detail and make sure nothing is left to chance.

We love our ways and our plans. We love being in control. But engaging the call of God on our lives is all about falling in love with His ways and plans and letting Him be in control. It's about rediscovering the reality that Adam and Eve walked away from and Jesus came to call us back to—that God's ways are higher, His plans are better, and He is in perfect control in every situation. But we can discover that only through stepping out and trusting Him.

One of the big things God does in the delay, which creates an essential opportunity for us to trust Him rather than ourselves, is to help us see where our expectations do not align with His. When He awakens our hearts to dream, our imagination naturally fills in a bunch of details about how and when things will go as we step out on the three-mile walk. However, very rarely do these details include delays in the timeline or things working out differently. Why? Because that's not how we would do things if we were in control. These details create expectations in our minds that don't necessarily line up with God's expectations, so when the journey doesn't live up to our expectations, we get frustrated and disappointed. Frustration and disappointment are the most obvious signs that our expectations are out of alignment with God's. This bring us to a point of decision. Will we allow our disappointment to lead us into bitterness and disillusionment? Sadly, many people choose this and shipwreck their lives as a result. Or will we allow God to align us with His expectations? Will we trust Him with the how, what, and when of our dreams? Trusting Him always leads to freedom and life.

The more we choose to trust God, the more we will come to share His perspective on seasons of delay and respond to them productively instead of grabbing for control or getting disappointed. In delay, God is forming us to be able to live from trust in Him so completely and consistently that we begin to exhibit two powerful character traits: *patient endurance* and *contented confidence*.

Patient Endurance

Shortly after we planted Jesus Culture Sacramento, we hit a tough financial spot. Though we had been around for years as a ministry, we became an independent organization when we planted the church, which brought challenges we had never faced with managing cash flow. With all the expenses of a new church and transition, cash was beyond tight, and we reached a point where it was going to run out in a few months. We did what we knew to do: we cut expenses and took it to God in prayer. But days turned into weeks and months without our seeing any significant shift in the situation. Whenever I prayed, the Lord kept bringing me back to James 1:4: "Let patience have its perfect work, that you may be perfect and complete, lacking nothing" (NKJV).

I need you to be patient, I heard Him speak to my heart. *I'm trying to release things to you. It is my kindness that you are in this delay. I am developing something in you. You are lacking something, and it is through patience that I'm going to give it to you.*

Patience doesn't come naturally to any of us, but I think we have a distinct disadvantage in our culture when it comes to practicing patience or discovering its value. Before today's technology, people were forced to learn patience, because that was the way the world operated. If you wanted to communicate with someone, you had to write or type a letter, mail it, wait for the letter to get there, and wait for the person to write back. This took a long time, especially if the person was overseas. If you wanted to buy something and they didn't have it at the store, you had to order it from a catalog and wait. I remember being part of a music club in which you had to wait for them to ship you an album after its release. I patiently waited for whatever new music was headed my way. Culture had more patience naturally built into it because everything moved slower. It was our only choice. Today, with email, smartphones, and Amazon Prime Now, everything is immediate, and as convenient as this delay reduction in our lives may feel, it has a downside. Studies have shown that technology, as great as it has been, has shortened our attention span and our ability to be patient, and even discouraged us from learning the value of patience and waiting.

The Bible says that when we allow patience to work on us, we become "perfect and complete, lacking nothing" (James 1:4 NKJV). There are things in our lives we are lacking, areas of immaturity and weakness where we need to be instructed, trained, equipped, and strengthened. When we don't see the spiritual significance of patience, we miss one of the delivery systems God uses to perfect us and make sure we lack nothing for our journey. God cares that we would be complete, mature, and lacking nothing, so in His kindness, He brings seasons of delay during which patience can go to work in our lives. Getting impatient and trying to rush the process only causes us to miss out on what we need. I want you to hear that again. Where patience is required, it is the kindness of God, who longs to release things to us so that we would lack nothing.

One day in the process of praying for our financial situation, the Holy Spirit gave me a picture that really helped me shift my perspective on the work of patience in my life. I heard Him say, *Banning, right now you're in the weight room. When this season is over and I put you in the game, you're going to be grateful for your time in the weight room.*

It was profound for me to realize that I wasn't even in the game yet! All we were walking through, individually and as a team, was preparation for something greater. This presented me with a choice: I could be frustrated with the weight room, where I was in discomfort, being stretched and having to grow, or I could be grateful because it was preparing me for what was ahead. I decided I didn't want to rush the time in the weight room and jump into the game before I was ready. I wanted to stay in the weight room as long as it took to get the strength I needed. God was strengthening my faith. He was growing my trust in Him. These were things I would need if I was going to not only thrive on the three-mile walk but experience the fullness of relationship God desires to bring me into.

God wants us to engage the wait of delay like weights at the gym—to leverage the tension of this time in a way that increases our strength and endurance. The word *patience* in James 1:4 is a translation of the Greek word *hypomone*, which means to "stay under" and is also translated "endurance," "steadfastness," "constancy," and "perseverance."[10] In the same way that lifting weights correctly makes us physically powerful, engaging the wait of delay makes us internally powerful and ready for what God has for us.

We see this power in the life of Jesus. The Scriptures show us how Christ stayed under the weight that the Father had asked Him to carry, and how this was the secret to His powerful authority and to His powerful ability to run His race to the end. When a centurion asked Jesus to heal his servant, he rightly recognized Jesus as a man *under* authority. "I also am a man placed under authority, having soldiers under me. And I say to one, 'Go,' and he goes; and to another, 'Come,' and he comes; and to my servant, 'Do this,' and he does it" (Luke 7:8 NKJV). It was because Jesus stayed under the Father's authority, refusing to do anything except what the Father was saying and doing, despite every demonic and human pressure to do otherwise, that He spoke and acted with the Father's authority to release the kingdom of God wherever He went. He also stayed under the Father's authority by submitting fully to His will, even to the point of the cross. "Abba, Father, all things are possible for You. Take this cup away from Me; nevertheless, not what I will, but what You will" (Mark 14:36 NKJV). He succeeded where every other human had failed in trusting the Father completely, and the powerful authority and endurance this produced in His life enabled Him to triumph over the devil and bring salvation to earth.

God wants to produce the same authority and endurance in our lives. We all want power to do what we're called to do, and we want to see God's power released through our lives, but we don't always understand that this power comes only through practicing patience in the delay—through God giving us opportunity after opportunity to trust Him by waiting on Him and surrendering to Him.

When I was in my twenties, a seasoned minister gave me an invaluable word of wisdom and warning. He said, "Your test is going to be whether you get ahead of God." This has proven to be true. Again and again, I have found myself wanting to accelerate beyond God's pace and timetable. The root of this impatience is always the issue of trust. One of the ongoing disciplines in my life has become checking in to see if I am following God at His pace and not rushing ahead because I don't trust His timetable.

One of the tensions I experienced as a young man was that I felt ready before I was. I knew I had a call on my life. I had a vision and I was running after it. But I hadn't spent time in the weight room yet; patience hadn't done enough work in my life to produce the authority and endurance I needed. Authority is when your words and actions carry weight; doors open, atmosphere shifts when you walk into the room, and heaven and hell know who you are. But our words and actions carry weight only after we have carried the weight in the weight room. Endurance is when you can outlast any obstacle and any opponent—when you're the most patient person in the room. But you become patient only by being patient.

The three-mile walk becomes so much more enjoyable when we understand that everything God is doing in the delay is pouring into our long-term stability and success. He wants us to have the weight-bearing capacity to share His power and glory and run our race to the end, just like Jesus. He doesn't want us to stay in a place of weakness, immaturity, and lack, where our trust can be shaken. The delay is where He establishes us with patient endurance.

Contented Confidence

When Jesus told Martha to believe, He told her what to believe in. "The one who believes *in me* will live" (John 11:25, emphasis added). The Christian life is not faith in a creed or doctrine; it is trust in the person of Jesus. Again, seasons of delay allow us to see who we really trust. I may say Jesus is all I need, that my identity is found in Him alone, and that He is my life's pursuit, not wealth, power, accomplishments, or recognition. But until that gets tested, I don't know if I truly believe that.

When Jesus Culture hit its first big season of growth, it was electric. We were just a youth group that decided to put on some conferences and record the times of worship. I was a youth pastor with a handful of youth leaders and some passionate young people. Then, all of a sudden, people around the world were listening to our worship music, our conferences were growing, and we were being invited onto stages that were bigger than we had ever experienced. But the pressure and attention that came with these things began to expose cracks in our world. Team relationships were being strained nearly to the breaking point.

I remember sitting on a tour bus in England, wrestling with what was happening. Each night on the tour, we were having powerful gatherings with hungry people, worshiping and seeking God with passion. It was beautiful to see what God was doing and what we were able to be a part of each night. Yet our team was struggling with so much interpersonal tension and anxiety that I wasn't sure we were going to make it. Would we survive this season of growth, or would it crush us? Would this ministry continue or die out as so many others had?

As I sat alone on that bus, I began to grapple with some big questions. *What if this all went away? Would I be okay if Jesus Culture ended today? Would I be okay if all these invitations to be onstage dried up and I ended up in hiddenness and obscurity?* That last question was tough for me; the influencer in me has a high need for significance and impact. As I weighed what this potential loss would mean for me, I remembered something Mike Bickle had said in a sermon series on the life of David. He had explained that David defined success as loving God and being loved by God. He was content hiding in the wilderness or reigning in the palace, because he could love and be loved by God in both places, and that was enough.

That's all I want too, I told the Lord. *Whether I am known or unknown, preaching to thousands or pastoring a group of ten kids, or wherever You lead me, all I want to do is be loved by You and love You. That is enough. That is success. If all this goes away, I will be fine, because I can love You anywhere.*

It was a marking moment in my life. I had always said that He was enough for me, but that truth became truer when it was tested. This choice to be content with Jesus deepened my confidence that I believed what I said I believed, and it reanchored my heart in Him as my source of significance, security, and strength.

Contentment is another quality that our culture doesn't appreciate; our culture even discourages it. We're a consumer culture with a scarcity mentality. As I mentioned earlier, in order to sell us products, businesses need us to be discontent with what we have, so that we will buy what they are offering. Even though we are the wealthiest society in history, we live with this constant anxiety that there's never enough and we're not enough. So much of what drives our busy, impatient culture is our frantic effort to find ful-fillment and security in everything but God, which only leads to more discontentment.

Augustine famously said, "You have made us for yourself, and our hearts are restless till they find their rest in thee." In the delay, God wants to lead us into this deep heart rest that can be found only in Him. He wants to show us that He is enough for us. To do that, He must expose where we are looking for contentment and confidence in other things. Paul said he had "learned to be content whatever the circumstances . . . in any and every situation, whether well fed or hungry, whether living in plenty or in want" (Phil. 4:11–12). This is what God does in the delay: He leads us through all kinds of circumstances so we can discover that He is enough in every single one. As a result, we gain the confidence that comes only through total dependence on Him. "I can do all things through Christ who strengthens me" (Phil. 4:13 NKJV).

Confidence is a wonderful word. It is boldness rooted in trust. When we take someone into our confidence, we share personal, intimate secrets with them. When that person reciprocates and protects that place of vulnerable trust, it gives us freedom to speak freely, to be ourselves, and to ask for what we need in the relation-ship. This vulnerability, intimacy, security, and freedom are what God wants to cultivate with us in the delay. Some of my most beautiful moments of intimacy with the Lord have occurred in the delay, because the delay is when I surrender to Him. Surrender is an act of trust and intimacy that gives God the opportunity to demonstrate once again how much He cares for me, how powerful and capable He is, and why trusting Him always leads to life. This deepens my confidence in Him and makes me confident to be and do what He has called me to be and do.

Graduation Is Coming

Seasons of delay are followed by moments of breakthrough and season shifts—those moments in the Bible that begin, "And suddenly . . ."

> When the Day of Pentecost had fully come, they were all with one accord in one place. *And suddenly* there came a sound from heaven, as of a rushing mighty wind, and it filled the whole house where they were sitting.
>
> —ACTS 2:1-2 NKJV (EMPHASIS ADDED)

> At midnight Paul and Silas were praying and singing hymns to God, and the prisoners were listening to them. *Suddenly* there was a great earthquake, so that the foundations of the prison were shaken; and immediately all the doors were opened and everyone's chains were loosed.
>
> —ACTS 16:25-26 NKJV (EMPHASIS ADDED)

> The Lord said, "Hear what the unjust judge said. And shall God not avenge His own elect who cry out day and night to Him, though He bears long with them? I tell you that He will avenge them *speedily*. Nevertheless, when the Son of Man comes, will He really find faith on the earth?"
>
> —LUKE 18:6-8 NKJV (EMPHASIS ADDED)

In the delay, God "bears long" with us, but when the breakthrough comes, it comes quickly. Again—and I can't stress this enough—just because you are in a bearing long season doesn't mean you are off course. Yes, sometimes the bearing long part seems like it will never end. But it will end. It's like having a newborn baby.

When Ellianna was a newborn, it felt like she was never going to sleep through the night. The weariness of staying up with her, night after night, seemed interminable. SeaJay and I would look at each other with that look of despair, thinking that this was our life now and it would never end. We couldn't do this for the next eighteen years. Then one night, at seven weeks, everything shifted, and Ellianna began to sleep through the night. I like to tell new parents, whom I recognize by their hollow eyes and look of stunned exhaustion, "Don't worry, the sleeplessness will end soon, and when it happens, everything will be okay. The shift will come."

This is why when we're going through a delay, the one thing we mustn't do is stop. It's tragic when people miss their "suddenly" moment because they stop in the season of delay. They never make it to their graduation. Education takes years and can be a grind, but then the day of graduation comes. In one short day, the season of education ends, you get a diploma, and you transition to a new season. Education may be long, but graduation is quick. This is what it's like going through delay; we mustn't stop until the breakthrough comes.

Typically, people give up before their breakthrough because they get confused, discouraged, or distracted. They don't see the delay as a season of training and education during which God wants to deepen their trust, so they don't lean into the tension and discomfort of the process. Or worse, they interpret the delay as an end. When the dreams of their hearts take longer than they thought or don't work out the way they expected, they decide that their dreams just aren't going to happen, that the story is over.

As a college student who knew I was called to preach, I listened to certain preachers and sermons as I worked in the admissions office, folding flyers. I wore out some of the cassette tapes, listening to particular sermons so many times. One of the sermons I wore out was by Charles Crabtree. I will never forget the point of his sermon: "Don't put a period where God has put a comma." He used the story of David losing his first son with Bathsheba, but the story of Lazarus illustrates this point as well. When Jesus came to the tomb of Lazarus, he instructed the people to remove the stone. Jesus could have supernaturally removed the stone in front of the tomb of Lazarus, but He required the mourners to do the job, because they were the ones who put it there. They had decided to put a period at the end of Lazarus's life because his story was over. According to Jesus, however, the story was not over. So often in a season of delay, we think the story is over. We think our dreams are dead and buried, and seal them in a tomb. We put a period where God has put only a comma. The story is not over, and God's not done. And when He comes and invites us to move forward with Him again, He will require us to remove every stone of hopelessness and unbelief so He can demonstrate once again that He is the God of resurrection.

I urge you: If you are going through a delay, keep going. Lean into Jesus. Trust Him. Allow Him to develop patient endurance and contented confidence in you. Also, surround yourself with believers who can help you gain godly perspective on your season. As questions like, "Don't You care?" "Where are You?" and "Why are You letting this happen?" come to the surface in this season, invite these other believers to speak truth over you and remind you that God is trustworthy and working in your life. Just because God seems distant, hidden, or hard to perceive in seasons of delay doesn't mean He's not working. I once heard someone say, "God is doing more behind your back than in front of your eyes." Even when you can't perceive Him, He is there. It's when we can't see that genuine faith is formed in us.

MILE 3

FAITH

FAITH NEVER KNOWS WHERE IT
IS BEING LED, BUT IT LOVES AND
KNOWS THE ONE WHO IS LEADING.

—Oswald Chambers

FAITH IS NOT SOMETHING THAT
GOES AGAINST THE EVIDENCE,
IT GOES BEYOND IT.

—Alister McGrath

8

CHAPTER

—

The Supply Line Strategy

Sometimes we read stories in Scripture from a distance. It doesn't fully connect with us that these stories really happened. There were real people who made real decisions and had real emotions in the midst of their journey. When I read the story of Jonathan taking on the army of the Philistines, I can't help but wonder what he was thinking. What was it that led Jonathan to believe that he and one other guy had what it took to go up against an entire outpost of Philistines? When Jonathan looked at the odds of success, why did he conclude they had a chance, when his father Saul and their six hundred men thought it was hopeless?

It wasn't just that Jonathan had set himself apart from the crowd to answer the call of God.

It wasn't just that he was a man of courage.

Jonathan saw possibilities where others saw impossibilities, because he had faith. He trusted God, and this trust defined the way he thought, felt, spoke, and acted. His whole perspective was shaped by what he knew about God's character, His covenant with His people, and how He had acted in power in the past to fulfill that covenant. Jonathan told his armor-bearer, "Come, let us go over to the garrison of these uncircumcised; it may be that the

LORD will work for us. For nothing restrains the LORD from saving by many or by few" (1 Sam. 14:6 NKJV). This is a statement of faith. Jonathan was saying, "I know who God is, I know what He can do, I know He's with me, and I know that if I step out with Him in this moment, He's going to be there with me."

Notice, Jonathan didn't say, "I know what God is going to do in this situation. He *will* work for us." Genuine faith isn't about being able to predict what God is going to do. It's about trusting Him and entrusting our lives to Him completely, knowing that whatever He will do is what we want to be partnering with. We see this faith in Shadrach, Meshach, and Abednego. When King Nebuchadnezzar commanded them to bow down to his idol on pain of death, they boldly declared, "If that is the case, our God whom we serve is able to deliver us from the burning fiery furnace, and He will deliver us from your hand, O king. But if not, let it be known to you, O king, that we do not serve your gods, nor will we worship the gold image which you have set up" (Dan. 3:17–18 NKJV). They essentially said, "God is able to deliver, He will deliver, and even if He doesn't, we're still going with Him." Esther said the same thing: "I will go to the king, which is against the law; and if I perish, I perish!" (Est. 4:16 NKJV). Likewise, Job said, "Though He slay me, yet will I trust Him" (Job 13:15 NKJV). Faith says, "I'm going on this journey with you, God, no matter the outcome, because I trust You."

The three-mile walk is a walk of faith from start to end. Faith anchors us in the unseen reality of who God is, what He says, what He is doing, who He says we are, and what He says is possible. Faith equips us to see differently, because we live from the unseen.

Faith is the substance of things hoped for, the evidence of things not seen.

—HEBREWS 11:1 NKJV

> By faith we understand that the worlds were framed by
> the word of God, so that the things which are seen were
> not made of things which are visible.
>
> —HEBREWS 11:3 NKJV

> We fix our eyes not on what is seen, but on what is unseen,
> since what is seen is temporary, but what is unseen is
> eternal.... For we live by faith, not by sight.
>
> —2 CORINTHIANS 4:18; 5:7

Only by living from this unseen reality can we see what God says is possible for us. This is why it's impossible to engage our calling without faith. Only by living from the unseen can we become who God is calling us to be and do what He's calling us to do.

Growing Our Faith

Jesus is our clearest picture of what it looks like to walk in faith. He lived fully from the unseen realm—the realm of communion with His Father, the realm of the Spirit, the realm of the kingdom. These were the realities that defined and energized His mission, His perspective, His heart, His words, and His actions. He didn't look to Rome or Herod or the high priest or His family to tell Him who He was. He didn't look to human knowledge of medicine or physics to explain things or tell Him what was possible. He lived from a higher authority, a higher reality. As a result, He frequently saw, said, and did things very differently than did the people around Him. He saw God differently, almost exclusively calling Him "Father." Where most people were trying to run from God's punishment or manipulate Him through good works, Jesus showed that God's heart was to draw near us with love and forgiveness and offer Himself to us freely and generously. Jesus, sharing the Father's heart, saw people very differently; He welcomed the poor, outcast, humble, and unimportant while criticizing the wealthy, religious, and powerful. He saw sickness, disease, and demonic torment as afflictions to be healed instead of punishment that was deserved because of sin. He expected the natural world, which had been made by the word of God, to respond to that word when He spoke it, telling storms to be quiet, trees to be fruitful, and waves to become a firm path for Him to cross. He saw humility as the path to greatness, and death as the path to life. All of this flowed from His faith.

Jesus also spoke about faith constantly, expected His disciples to have it, corrected them when they didn't, and acknowledged it wherever He encountered it. In many of these instances, Jesus discussed faith in terms of degrees; He called people out when their faith was either little or great.

> "If God so clothes the grass of the field, which today is, and tomorrow is thrown into the oven, will He not much more clothe you, O you of *little faith*?"
> —MATTHEW 6:30 NKJV (EMPHASIS ADDED)

> When Jesus heard it, He marveled, and said to those who followed, "Assuredly, I say to you, I have not found such *great faith*, not even in Israel!"
> —MATTHEW 8:10 NKJV (EMPHASIS ADDED)

> He said to them, "Why are you fearful, O you of *little faith*?" Then He arose and rebuked the winds and the sea, and there was a great calm.
> —MATTHEW 8:26 NKJV (EMPHASIS ADDED)

Immediately Jesus stretched out His hand and caught him, and said to him, "O you of *little faith*, why did you doubt?"

—MATTHEW 14:31 NKJV (EMPHASIS ADDED)

Jesus answered and said to her, "O woman, *great* is your *faith*! Let it be to you as you desire." And her daughter was healed from that very hour.

—MATTHEW 15:28 NKJV (EMPHASIS ADDED)

Jesus, being aware of it, said to them, "O you of *little faith*, why do you reason among yourselves because you have brought no bread?"

—MATTHEW 16:8 NKJV (EMPHASIS ADDED)

Jesus said to them, "... Assuredly, I say to you, if you have *faith as a mustard seed*, you will say to this mountain, 'Move from here to there,' and it will move; and nothing will be impossible for you."

—MATTHEW 17:20 NKJV (EMPHASIS ADDED)

I think we all, as believers, want to have great faith, not little faith. Yet when we look at Jesus or men and women of great faith, it can feel daunting. We know we don't yet measure up to their level of conviction, confidence, and boldness in God. We know we don't yet perceive things and respond the way they do. But there's good news about faith: like everything else on the three-mile walk, growing our faith is a process. And there are a few simple truths we need to understand about faith and how it grows.

First, we all have a measure of faith. "God has dealt to each one a measure of faith" (Rom. 12:3 NKJV). The writer of Hebrews describes the kind of entry-level faith we need to start the journey. We must come to God with the confident belief not only that He exists but that He is "a rewarder of those who diligently seek Him" (Heb. 11:6 NKJV). Without this confidence, "it is impossible to please Him" (Heb. 11:6 NKJV). The beautiful thing is that God puts this belief in us! Jesus said, "No one can come to Me unless the Father who sent Me draws him" (John 6:44 NKJV). If we have come to Jesus and put our trust in Him as our Lord and Savior, it is because the Father has been shaping our heart with the awareness that He is real and that He will reward our pursuit of Him. This is how incredible God is: He essentially says, "You can't please me without faith, so I'm going to make sure you have faith." He gives us what we need to be successful.

Second, even if our faith is small, it is still powerful. Jesus said that just a mustard seed of faith is powerful enough to move mountains. You can't get much smaller than a mustard seed. The point Jesus was making is that whatever mountain is in your life, whatever impossible situation you find yourself facing, you can move it with the faith you have, if you use it.

That's the third thing we need to understand about faith: it becomes active and grows when we use it. In Ephesians 6, Paul describes faith as a shield "with which you will be able to quench all the fiery darts of the wicked one" (Eph. 6:16 NKJV). A shield is a weapon that works only when you wield it. Whatever we use, whatever we steward, grows and develops. As with a muscle in my body, if I do not use my faith, it atrophies and grows weak. The more I use it, the stronger and more effective my faith becomes.

Last, we get to ask for help. When the father of a demon-possessed child came to Jesus for help, "Jesus said to him, 'If you can believe, all things are possible to him who believes.' Immediately the father of the child cried out and said with tears, 'Lord, I believe;

help my unbelief!'" (Mark 9:23–24 NKJV). If we know our faith is small, we just need to ask God to grow our faith. If He gave us faith to begin with, we can be confident that He wants to give us more! Remember, the reward comes to those who diligently seek God. He wants us to keep coming back to Him, expecting Him to respond again and again as a good Father does.

Supply Line Strategy

Jesus said nothing is impossible for those who believe. Paul said that with faith we can extinguish not some but all of the fiery darts of the enemy. John said that our faith overcomes the world (1 John 5:4). When our faith is fully operational, the world, the flesh, and the devil don't stand a chance.

The enemy knows he can't win against our faith, so he organizes covert missions to penetrate our interior world, find our points of weakness, and disable us from within. He works to find places where he can cut off the internal supply lines to our faith.

Every army needs supplies—meals, munitions, and medicine—to stay in the battle. Thus they must develop a supply line strategy to keep these basic needs met, while protecting themselves from the enemy, who will work to cut off that supply line. Cutting off supply lines is the key strategy in attrition warfare, where the enemy wears you down to the point of collapse, through continuous loss of personnel and supplies, or in siege or blockade warfare, where the enemy builds barriers or sets up lines of defense to keep you from receiving supplies. If the enemy can cut off the supply line, they win the battle. Our enemy uses both types of warfare to attack the supply lines to faith in our lives. He tries to attack and chip away at the supplies we have while cutting us off from anything that would replenish our stores.

Two of the essential supplies we need for faith to be fully operational in our lives are *hope* and *peace*. To be successful on this three-mile walk, we must establish a strategy for building up, protecting, and replenishing these internal resources that fuel faith. We must learn how to import a steady flow of hope and peace into our hearts while preventing the enemy from sabotaging them.

Hope—Faith's Pilot Light

Our house has a gas fireplace. It's so convenient. All I have to do is push a button to start the flow of gas, and when the gas hits the pilot light, the fire ignites. When we bought the house, however, it was right before summer and I knew we wouldn't need the fireplace for a good four or five months, so I turned the pilot light off. When the weather began to get colder in the fall, I tried to relight the pilot light so we could start the fire. As much as I tried, however, I could not figure out how to keep the pilot light burning. I finally called a technician, who came to our house and not only lit the pilot light but taught me how to do it properly.

Hope is the pilot light in our hearts that ignites our faith. "Faith is the substance of things *hoped* for, the evidence of things not seen" (Heb. 11:1 NKJV, emphasis added). If we want to live with active and constantly growing faith, then we need to live with the continual presence of hope burning in our hearts. David said, "I will hope continually, and will praise You yet more and more" (Ps. 71:14 NKJV). As long as the pilot light of hope is lit, faith can be ignited in our lives.

Biblical hope is much more substantial and specific than wishful thinking, which is what most people mean when they say, "I hope so." Biblical hope is the joyful and confident expectation of good both now and in the future. To hope is to wait with expectation for good to come. Specifically, the good we are to wait for is God and all He has promised to us as His adopted sons and daughters. Paul prayed that our spiritual eyes would be open to see the unseen reality of "the hope of His calling, . . . the riches of the glory of His inheritance in the saints, and . . . the exceeding greatness of His power toward us who believe" (Eph. 1:18–19 NKJV). Seeing this unseen reality shows us what we are to wait for and joyfully expect. Assuming this posture of hope prepares us to activate faith to partner with God and what He's doing in our present situation.

No matter what we may be feeling in the moment, our hope is alive and well. The hope of the Christian life is a "living hope" (1 Peter 1:3) that both anchors our soul to eternal reality (Heb. 6:18–19) and causes us to abound with hope, as Paul prayed: "May the God of hope fill you with all joy and peace in believing, that you may abound in hope by the power of the Holy Spirit" (Rom. 15:13 NKJV). This means that Christians should have the most hope, and be the most consistently hopeful, of everyone on the planet. Hope should be not only evident in every area of our lives but abundantly evident. We should also be the people moving toward the future with the greatest confidence and momentum. Jeremiah 29:11 says, "I know the thoughts that I think toward you, says the LORD, thoughts of peace and not of evil, to give you a future and a hope" (NKJV). The more we learn God's thoughts and see from His perspective, the more we will believe we have a great future and continue to move toward it, even through difficulty and loss, for we are even called to grieve with hope. In the darkest times in our lives, the pilot light of hope remains lit. Paul wrote, "I do not want you to be ignorant, brethren, concerning those who have fallen asleep, lest you sorrow as others who have no hope" (1 Thess. 4:13 NKJV). No matter how bleak the situation or how devastating the loss, our living hope, which is ultimately the hope of resurrection life itself in Christ, buoys us even in sorrow and keeps us moving forward. We grieve differently because of the hope we have.

Unfortunately, many Christians do not abound with hope. Many struggle to live even a few notches above the level of hopelessness of the world around us. This should not be. We live in a wider culture that has bought into the enemy's lie that reality is basically meaningless and without purpose, so all we can do is attempt to invest it with some manmade purpose by filling our lives with pleasure, power, achievement, and accumulation. This worldview (secular materialism and progressivism) attacks our innate hope for eternal meaning and purpose and promotes a lifestyle that ultimately can produce only deep dissatisfaction, anxiety, and despair. We, as believers, are called to hold out hope to the world, but so many of us seem to be languishing under the hopelessness of our culture. There is a war over your hope. We've allowed ourselves to be cut off from the supply line of hope by aligning with the spirit of the age.

The author of Hebrews writes, "We desire that each one of you show the same diligence to the full assurance of hope until the end, that you do not become sluggish, but imitate those who through faith and patience inherit the promises" (Heb. 6:11–12 NKJV). The word diligence in this context means "haste," while the word sluggish means "slow." We are to live with an urgency about keeping hope in our lives; it's not something we can afford to get lazy about. This means we must daily practice spiritual warfare by renewing our minds with truth and confronting every lie that seeks to gain a place of influence in our beliefs and perspective. Hopelessness is a dead giveaway that we are believing lies. Again, as my friend Steve Backlund often says, "Any thought in our minds that is not sparkling with confident hope indicates that it is under the influence of a lie." You are not meant to live hopeless and must refuse to remain in that place. You are not powerless and can do something about it. On a regular basis, we must ask ourselves, "What am I believing about the future of my family? My finances? My career? My health? My relationships? Am I filled with a joyful, confident expectation and desire for good, or am I struggling with a lingering sense of anxiety or dread?" If we see any areas where we feel unease or dread, we need to invite the Holy Spirit to shine His light of truth on our hearts and expose the lies we are believing.

We also need to be feeding ourselves a steady diet of truth by reading, studying, meditating on, praying, and declaring the Word of God, which we can do in many forms and venues—privately with our Bibles and study tools, in small groups, at church, on our smartphones, or in a more formal setting like Bible or ministry school. The telltale sign that this diet is truly being metabolized is that we begin to overflow with hope in what is unseen, not in what is seen. As Paul writes, "Hope that is seen is no hope at all. Who hopes for what they already have? But if we hope for what we do not yet have, we wait for it patiently" (Rom. 8:24–25). Likewise, we overflow with hope in God Himself, not in any human solution. As David exhorts himself, "Why are you cast down, O my soul? And why are you disquieted within me? Hope in God; for I shall yet praise Him, the help of my countenance and my God" (Ps. 43:5 NKJV). Our hope is rooted entirely in God's faithfulness. Hebrews 10:23 says, "Let us hold fast the confession of our hope without wavering, for He who promised is faithful" (NKJV). We aren't looking for other things to save us, fulfill us, or supply what we need. We're not even looking to God's promises themselves. We're looking to Him, the one who promised. Only when our hope is anchored in God will it stay burning continually.

Last, we keep the pilot light of hope burning in our hearts by persevering. Yes, it takes hope to persevere. But the more we persevere—particularly, when we persevere until the breakthrough—the more hope becomes established in our lives. Paul writes, "We also glory in tribulations, knowing that tribulation produces perseverance; and perseverance, character; and character, hope. Now hope does not disappoint, because the love of God has been poured out in our hearts by the Holy Spirit who was given to us" (Rom. 5:3–5 NKJV).

The word tribulations here means "pressure." Living from the unseen creates pressure and tension in our lives because we are positioning ourselves in the conflict between the kingdom of heaven and the kingdom of this world. If we persevere, or stay under the pressure by aligning with the kingdom of God and remaining faithful to Him, who He's called us to be, and what He's called us to do, it produces proven character. The root Greek word for character is *dokimos*. In his commentary on the book of Romans, Donald Grey Barnhouse notes,

> In the ancient world there was no banking system as we know it today, and no paper money. All money was made from metal, heated until liquid, poured into moulds and allowed to cool. When the coins were cooled, it was necessary to smooth off the uneven edges. The coins were comparatively soft, and of course many people shaved them closely. In one century, more than eighty laws were passed in Athens to stop the practice of whittling down the coins then in circulation. But some money-changers were men of integrity, who would accept no counterfeit money; they were men of honour who put only genuine, full-weight money into circulation. Such men were called *dokimos*, and this word is used here for the Christian as he is to be seen by the world.[11]

When we have proven character, we're the real deal. We can look at ourselves and say, "God, You are faithful to Your Word. You brought me through this pressure, and it's shown that what You've put in my heart is real and not some fleeting fantasy. I am being who You've called me to be and doing what You've called me to do." Others can look at us and say, "Wow, God is real. That person proves that the hope of the gospel gives them the power to live completely differently than the world." This is why proven character produces hope—the joyful, confident expectation of coming good—that does not disappoint! Who we are becoming in the waiting proves that what we are waiting for is real, powerful, transformative, and worthy. And that keeps us supplied with hope, positioning us to keep waiting and staying ready to activate our faith in every situation.

Peace—Anchored in the Presence of Jesus

If faith is ignited in hope, it is anchored in peace. Biblical peace, like hope, is something more specific and substantial than worldly peace, which typically means the absence of conflict or chaos. Biblical peace—*shalom*—is the presence of safety, wholeness, and rest that comes only from being fully connected to and reliant on the source of those things, God Himself.

One of the most powerful pictures of this peace, and its relationship to faith, is the story of Jesus sleeping on the boat in a storm, then calming that storm with a word.

> That day when evening came, he said to his disciples, "Let us go over to the other side." Leaving the crowd behind, they took him along, just as he was, in the boat. There were also other boats with him. A furious squall came up,

and the waves broke over the boat, so that it was nearly swamped. Jesus was in the stern, sleeping on a cushion. The disciples woke him and said to him, "Teacher, don't you care if we drown?"

He got up, rebuked the wind and said to the waves, "Quiet! Be still!" Then the wind died down and it was completely calm.

He said to his disciples, "Why are you so afraid? Do you still have no faith?"

They were terrified and asked each other, "Who is this? Even the wind and the waves obey him!"

—MARK 4:35–41

Jesus slept in the storm and had authority over the storm because even though the storm was all around Him, it was not in Him. His heart was anchored in the unseen reality of heaven, which reigns over the chaos and darkness of earth. When I'm flying over an ocean and look down to see storm clouds, I often think of the boats that are experiencing the storms below. As I mentioned before, my experience on the ocean, even with small waves, has felt unbearable. The contrast between being tossed by the waves in a storm and calmly flying over the storm is a tangible picture for me of what it's like to live from peace like Jesus did. Peace is an internal reality that we can not only live from amid chaos and conflict but also be empowered by to face and overcome chaos and conflict.

The disciples in this story, however, were not just being tossed by the waves externally; they were in chaos internally. What was happening around them was a picture of what was happening inside them. They were anxious, worried, and terrified. Fear, worry, and anxiety cripple our faith, which is why Scripture is full of admonitions not to be afraid, worried, or anxious. Of course, the sheer number of times we are told, "Fear not" shows us that God understands that we all deal with fear, worry, and anxiety. He doesn't want us to beat ourselves up or worry because we worry! He simply wants to remind us that we have the power to stop being afraid and to stop worrying, and show us how to shift from fear and worry to peace.

In the same way that hopelessness is a sign that we are believing lies, worry is a sign that we are looking to something or someone besides God as our source of security and sustenance. The path out of worry and into faith is the path of reanchoring our hearts in His provision, protection, and presence. A good place to start is by remembering what He has promised is ours as beloved sons and daughters:

> He said to His disciples, "Therefore I say to you, do not worry about your life, what you will eat; nor about the body, what you will put on. Life is more than food, and the body is more than clothing. Consider the ravens, for they neither sow nor reap, which have neither storehouse nor barn; and God feeds them. Of how much more value are you than the birds? And which of you by worrying can add one cubit to his stature? If you then are not able to do the least, why are you anxious for the rest? Consider the lilies, how they grow: they neither toil nor spin; and yet I say to you, even Solomon in all his glory was not arrayed like one of these. If then God so clothes the grass, which today is in the field and tomorrow is thrown into the oven, how much more will He clothe you, O you of little faith?
>
> "And do not seek what you should eat or what you should drink, nor have an anxious mind. For all these things the nations of the world seek after, and your Father knows that you need these things. But seek the kingdom of God, and all these things shall be added to you.

Do not fear, little flock, for it is your Father's good
pleasure to give you the kingdom."
—LUKE 12:22–32 NKJV

There are so many things our Father knows we need and has already taken care of for us. I was chatting once with a friend who had moved from overseas with his family. When we moved our family to Sacramento, I asked him what he had learned about moving his family, and he said, "I wish I hadn't worried about the things God had already taken care of." I knew I had been doing exactly that. I decided to take some time and write down everything I was worrying about. At the top, I wrote, "Things God Has Already Taken Care Of." There wasn't one thing I was worrying about that didn't fit on that list, nothing that His promises of provision, protection, and presence didn't cover. Making the list shifted my heart into a place of peace and rest in Him as my source.

Ever since then, whenever I am struggling under the weight of worry, I make these lists. They're one way I practice what Paul teaches us in Philippians: "Be anxious for nothing, but in everything by prayer and supplication, with thanksgiving, let your requests be made known to God; and the peace of God, which surpasses all understanding, will guard your hearts and minds through Christ Jesus" (Phil. 4:6–7 NKJV). After we remember God's promises, we need to take everything we're anxious about to Him in prayer and give it all to Him, putting our trust in Him as our source. We can always tell we've successfully made this exchange, because we feel that the burden on our hearts is lifted and replaced with His peace. It's "the peace that passes understanding" because we can receive and experience it without needing answers or reasons. Many times, we get caught up thinking that we need an explanation for what we're going through or how things are going to work out for the good. But peace isn't found in answers or knowing what's ahead. It's found only in the presence of the Prince of Peace. "He Himself is our peace" (Eph. 2:14 NKJV).

Jesus expected His disciples to have peace because He was in the boat with them. It's the presence of Jesus, not the absence of storms, that anchors our hearts in peace. Jesus led His disciples into that storm, and on our three-mile walk, He will lead us into storms too. How else can we learn that the one who overcomes the storms is always with us and lives inside us and has given us all we need to have peace in the chaos? Jesus says, "These things I have spoken to you, that in Me you may have peace. In the world you will have tribulation; but be of good cheer, I have overcome the world" (John 16:33 NKJV).

Jesus paid a massive price for us to live and walk in His peace. "He was wounded for our transgressions, He was bruised for our iniquities; the chastisement for our peace was upon Him, and by His stripes we are healed" (Isa. 53:5 NKJV). The cross reconciled us to God, enabling us to live again in the deep security of His presence, provision, and protection. All we need to do is access this ability in relational exchanges with Him. We recently took our kids to SeaWorld and got all-inclusive tickets that covered food, drinks, passes to get to the front of the lines, and more. After walking for miles and riding as many rollercoasters as possible, my kids began complaining about being hungry. I had already explained to them that their ticket included food, but apparently they hadn't gotten it, so I explained it again. All my kids had to do was go up to the food counters and show their tickets to access everything that had been purchased. That's what it's like on the three-mile walk. Everything we need for the journey has already been purchased. If we're lacking peace, all we have to do is go to Jesus and ask for it.

The most important thing we can do to keep the peace supplied in our lives is to stay aware of the presence of Jesus with us. We are never alone on this three-mile walk, and the one who is with us is constantly available and inviting us to hand our burdens to Him and receive His provision and protection in return. Putting our hearts at rest in His presence positions us to step out in faith, knowing that we are fully backed, supplied, and surrounded by Him.

Spiritual Disciplines

Throughout the Gospels, we see Jesus, the perfecter of our faith, practicing spiritual disciplines like studying, discussing, and praying the Scriptures, engaging in all forms of public and private prayer, fasting, feasting, silence, solitude, and more. Unfortunately, many Christians perceive spiritual disciplines as religious rituals and either don't engage them or kind of go through the motions of prayer, reading the Bible, attending church, or singing worship songs. Spiritual disciplines, when used properly, are our supply line strategy for keeping our eyes fixed on unseen reality and keeping our hearts anchored in the presence of God so that we are receiving a continual supply of hope and peace to fuel our faith. We are called to be diligent in this. In the next chapter, we'll take a closer look at some of the underlying principles of how spiritual disciplines work, as we explore one of the most important ways we engage and grow our faith on the three-mile walk: the practice of thanksgiving.

9

—

Thankful in the Middle Seat

I love being the pastor of Jesus Culture Sacramento. Leading a local church community is one of the great joys and privileges of my life. Every week that we gather, I love to see our people's passion for one another, and their hunger for the presence and the Word of God. Easily, it is my favorite place to preach.

Shortly after we launched our church, a reporter from our local paper visited us on a Sunday and wrote an article about his experience at our service. He had heard about what was happening with us and was intrigued; he wanted to learn more. At the weekly staff meeting, our team and I read the article, which was very positive and encouraging. The reporter had great things to say and was very kind in how he described our church. When he came to describing my sermon, the word he used was *homespun*. That's not really a word I hear often, and so out of curiosity, I decided to look up the definition. It means "simple and unsophisticated." When I read the definition to our team, they laughed for a few minutes. The writer wasn't saying it in negative light, but it was interesting to hear his experience.

Oddly enough, I was encouraged by someone experiencing my

sermon as simple and unsophisticated. I think we tend to compli- cate things Jesus made simple. When I coach basketball, I often tell players, "Don't make an easy shot hard." If they have a straight line to the basket for an easy layup, they don't need to add in a bunch of dribbling and do a reverse layup. I'm not saying we shouldn't study or wrestle with the things that are complicated in our walk with God, but we don't need to add complexity where Jesus gave us simplicity.

One of the things I see believers complicate unnecessarily is the will of God. People tie themselves in knots trying to figure out what God's will for their lives is, whether they're doing His will, or how to pray according to His will. Yes, there are many moments in our lives when we don't see the path ahead and must ask God for wisdom, discernment, and guidance on how to move forward. But there are some things we can do without having to wonder if we're aligned with His will, because Scripture clearly tells us it is. One of those is found in 1 Thessalonians 5:18, where Paul writes, "In everything give thanks; for this is the will of God in Christ Jesus for you" (NKJV). It's fairly simple. In everything, we are to give thanks. We'd find that so many issues in our lives would sort themselves out if we simply followed the command to give thanks.

Thankfulness is an essential spiritual practice on the three- mile walk. It is a supply line strategy for importing hope, peace, joy, and every other faith-fueling resource we need, because it works to keep our eyes fixed on the unseen, our heart anchored to God's heart, and our perspective aligned with eternal truth, which is the posture we need to live from to operate in faith. Again, faith is all about staying connected to the greater reality of the kingdom of God. This doesn't mean ignoring, diminishing, or denying visible reality. Faith moves mountains not by pretending they aren't there or aren't mountains but by recognizing there is a greater power than those mountains. Jonathan didn't set out to confront the Philistines by pretending they didn't exist or weren't a threat. He framed that threat with the perspective of a man and a warrior who knew that the God of Israel was with him and for him. Faith sees what is seen from the perspective of the unseen.

Continually giving thanks in every situation gives us eyes of faith. Specifically, it helps us to see God's bigger purpose in times of trial, to see the power of persevering in prayer, and to see the realm of abundance we are connected to as the Father's sons and daughters. Seeing with this perspective positions us to act with faith in every circumstance.

See the Promotion

On our team and throughout our organization, we are intentional about the culture we are creating. I believe that the health and effectiveness of any team is connected to its culture. For this reason, we spend a lot of time communicating the core values and practices we want to define our environment, and ways to make sure everyone on the team has fully bought into them. We created a booklet with nine core values and thirteen practices, and we give this booklet to every team member and review it regularly. One of the thirteen practices is called "We Find Joy Even in the Middle Seat."

This title refers to an experience I had on a flight from California to New York City. When you fly as much as I do, you gain status on airlines and become accustomed to either being upgraded or getting the seat you want. This trip was last-minute, however, and the only seat left on the flight was the worst seat on the plane—a middle seat in the very last row, with limited legroom and no ability to recline, because of the bathroom wall behind it. When I got to the seat and realized I was going to be spending the next five hours crammed between two people, I started to feel irritated and annoyed. Then, about five minutes into my pity party, I stopped myself, because I realized how ridiculous my attitude was. Over the years, I've studied much of church and revival history. I've read hundreds of stories of men and women who have sacrificed everything for the gospel, and I know many people around the world who are currently enduring all kinds of discomfort to bring the good news to the world. Not to be dramatic for the sake of being dramatic, but I am part of a lineage of faith in which people have been burned at the stake because of their commitment to put Scripture in the hands of others, have died trying to reach tribes that had never heard the name of Jesus, and have sold everything to move to China to start an orphanage for kids who were disabled and unwanted, so these children could be loved for the time they had on this earth. And there I was, sitting in the middle seat, annoyed that I had to be inconvenienced for five hours to do what God has called me to do. Even as I write this, I'm embarrassed to think about how easily I can lose perspective, become ungrateful, and feel entitled about things as trivial as a seat on an airplane. It's so easy to slip into an attitude of ungratefulness and grumbling, and when that happens, I lose the perspective needed to operate in faith.

The practice of finding joy even in the middle seat is about keeping a perspective of gratitude in every situation we find ourselves in. It's about staying anchored in the reality that everything we get to do on this three-mile walk with God is the honor and privilege of a lifetime. Although we may walk through difficult situations, thankfulness allows us to recognize that problems are opportunities for God to show up, so we face them with optimism and joy.

Paul doesn't say that we are to be thankful only in the easy situations; he says we are also to be thankful in the difficult ones. When things are easy, comfortable, and pleasurable, it's easy to be thankful. But being thankful even when there is pressure allows us to find heaven's perspective on our situation so we can approach it with eyes of faith. It was during my most difficult season of ministry that the following passages of Scripture came alive for me like never before.

> My brethren, count it all joy when you fall into various trials, knowing that the testing of your faith produces patience. But let patience have its perfect work, that you may be perfect and complete, lacking nothing. If any of you lacks wisdom, let him ask of God, who gives to all liberally and without reproach, and it will be given to him. But let him ask in faith, with no doubting, for he who doubts is like a wave of the sea driven and tossed by the wind.
>
> —JAMES 1:2–6 NKJV

> In this you greatly rejoice, though now for a little while, if need be, you have been grieved by various trials, that the genuineness of your faith, being much more precious than gold that perishes, though it is tested by fire, may be found to praise, honor, and glory at the revelation of Jesus Christ.
>
> —1 PETER 1:6–7 NKJV

When I say these verses came alive for me, I don't mean it was comfortable. They pierced my heart. I knew I was going through a trial. The pressure was intense. Things were imploding all around me, and it was not fun. I was having a hard time sleeping at night. I also knew I was not counting it all joy or greatly rejoicing. At best,

I was putting my head down and trying to just push through. I had no idea how I was supposed to shift from just surviving this trial to rejoicing in it. I definitely was not thankful for it. But I knew that was what I needed to do, so I asked the Holy Spirit to work in my heart and change my perspective. Could I be thankful even in the midst of this trial?

The Lord started helping me see right by having me unpack the word *trial*. We often call struggles, difficulties, and challenges trials without thinking about what that word means. A trial is the act of trying, testing, or proving something to ascertain results. A criminal trial in court determines whether someone is guilty or innocent of a crime, on the basis of evidential proof. A clinical trial tests medicines, studies their effects, and makes sure they are safe enough before releasing them to the public. Athletes perform time trials to qualify for competition. Cars perform crash tests to see how their integrity will hold up under pressure. A trial exposes authenticity, integrity, and readiness, and where those things are lacking.

Peter calls our faith "much more precious than gold." When our faith is tested in fire, God is trying to reveal to us that our faith is genuine. Before the promotion that is coming, God wants to show us that we have the authenticity, integrity, and readiness to step into the coming assignment. From His perspective, a trial is a very good and necessary thing. I was surviving the trial rather than rejoicing in it and being thankful for it, because I didn't understand it was the last necessary step before I transitioned into the next season. I don't think I'm alone in this; I've known many friends who have gone through difficult transitions and struggled to understand why things were so hard, only to realize later that they were simply taking their final exam at the end of their current season before graduating to the next season. Thankfulness allows us to see seasons correctly.

So often we complain, grumble, and are ungrateful about a trial when God is saying, *I'm trying to show you that your faith is pure, genuine gold. I'm trying to show you that you know what's on this test. I'm trying to build your trust, confidence, and anticipation for what we're going to do next on the journey.* In trials, God is trying to show us things we need to know about ourselves and Him. He already knows the truth about us—that we're ready for this trial—but we need to know it on a deeper level. Truth needs to be tested in order for us to really know and believe it. Only tested truth can anchor us to eternal reality.[12]

I'm not a rock climber, but I enjoy watching rock climbing documentaries. Once I get past the anxiety of seeing someone dangling thousands of feet up a rock wall, there is something inspiring about watching the passion and dedication of these people to go out in nature, test their limits, and do the exhilarating and difficult work required to climb that rock. One of the things rock climbers use to be successful and safe in their climbs are anchors to secure themselves to a rock face. Professional climbers are trained in how to look for natural anchors in the rock, as well as how to use artificial anchors like spring-loaded camming devices, aluminum chalk stones, steel expansion bolts, and pitons. When climbers have tested these anchors to make sure they are secure, they are able to relax and climb up vertical surfaces with confidence, knowing that if they slip and fall, the anchor will hold them.

In the same way, there's a confidence that comes to us when truths become anchor points in our lives because they have been tested. There is a freedom we experience when we are secure in these truths, a freedom to climb, knowing the truths we are anchored to will hold. We are able to advance with power and purpose to the next level God has for us on this three-mile walk.

When we are thankful in all things, we see God's purpose even in our trials, and it becomes much easier to rejoice in them. It's easy to repeat the truth that God will never leave you or forsake you. But when you walk out that truth, it becomes an anchor in your life. When you are facing a situation that is overwhelming, difficult, and scary and you experience the faithfulness of a Father who is with you every step of the way, that truth becomes an anchor. People who have gone through the fire and have had God stand with them in the midst of that come out the other side with a confidence that God will never leave them or forsake them. This was the truth that became firm in my life through that difficult season, and I am eternally grateful for it. I find myself praying often, "Thank You, God, for allowing me to walk out what I believe."

See Power in Persistence

As I mentioned in chapter 7, our first couple years in Sacramento had seasons of financial strain. Part of the weight I was lifting in the weight room during that season of delay was the possibility that we would have to cut staff salaries for a time. We had all stepped out in faith together to follow God, and we had seen Him do amazing things and provide in incredible ways. Yet there we were, facing the real possibility that our cash was about to run out if we didn't make some hard decisions that could affect our team and their families.

Near the beginning of this ordeal, I was sitting in an airplane, flying home from a trip, when God spoke to my heart. *I want to teach your team the power of prayer.* So we started gathering daily as a team to pray and press in for financial breakthrough and provision. Thus began what someone soon dubbed "Prayer o'Clock" at the Jesus Culture office. Every workday at 10:00 a.m., everyone stopped what they were working on and gathered to pray for fifteen minutes. Sometimes the prayer was powerful, and sometimes it was boring, but we stuck with it.

As we prayed through the summer and into the fall, we began to see small breakthroughs—donations or unexpected income that came in and pushed out farther the projection of when we would run out of cash. We rejoiced and continued to pray, but as we neared late fall, even though the projections were later in the year than we had originally thought, we were still on track to run out of cash. Our senior team met and decided that by a certain date, we would need to cut salaries by a certain percentage for a few months to bridge the gap. I didn't want to do this, especially because the holidays were coming up, when people needed more money. In the history of Jesus Culture, we had never had to cut salaries. But no other solution seemed viable, so I sent an email to the staff to let them know this might be coming and to be prepared. I explained that it wasn't certain and we were still praying, but they needed to be aware that it could happen.

That November, just a week before we had to make the final call on whether to cut salaries, we traveled to England for our annual conference in Manchester. We love England and all that God is doing there, but the conference couldn't have come at a worse time financially, because we already knew we were going to lose money on it, right during our projected cash flow shortage. We continued to gather every day and pray as a team, waiting to see what God would do.

The conference was powerful; thousands of people came together to seek and worship God with passion, and many experienced breakthroughs and marking moments. In three days of meetings, we took only one offering and had a certain number we needed to come in so we would not lose more than we were planning on already. I walked off the stage that night after taking the offering and could feel that it had fallen flat. I wasn't confident we would even get the budgeted number we had for the offering. But after the service, a man approached me and asked if we could talk. He explained that God had spoken to him, and he wanted to partner with us financially. He believed in what we were doing, and he said he had a mandate to help build the house of God, a place for people to encounter the presence of God. The amount God had told him to donate was the amount we needed to cover the loss of the conference, and it was the very thing we needed to keep us from having to cut salaries.

We came home from England rejoicing that God had taken care of our team. However, while I was glad we didn't have to cut salaries, I was still sad that we were not going to be able to give year-end bonuses to our staff. Then, just one day before our annual Christmas staff party, where we traditionally hand out the bonuses, I met with a man at our office who said he wanted to give us a year-end gift. The amount covered all the bonuses for our entire team.

I can so easily be ungrateful about these seasons that are difficult and stretching, but it became clear that God was doing something incredible with our team through it. Just as He told me, He was teaching us a focused, invaluable lesson on the power of persistent prayer. We learned that seeing our challenges with a faith perspective doesn't mean expecting that only "one and done" prayer is required. It means persisting in the posture of prayer until we see the mountain move. That season of prayer built faith into our foundation, and this faith continues to shape how we pray for greater provision and breakthrough.

After that season, I began to look at difficult situations, even in my family, from a different perspective. If you spend any length of time around our family, you learn quickly that my wife and kids love pets. Some time ago my daughter Raya, who was sixteen, began asking us for a cat. We already had dogs and rabbits, and I didn't want another animal in our home, but she was so persistent that we finally relented and got her a cat for Christmas. She immediately fell in love with it.

There was just one problem. One of our dogs didn't like the cat. It regularly growled at the cat and twice attacked it, which devastated Raya and stressed out the whole family. We started keeping the dog on a leash when the cat was roaming around the house, and we researched methods for creating peace and harmony between our pets, but nothing we tried worked. I didn't know what to do. Getting rid of either pet wasn't an option; that would crush my kids. But I also refused to allow our house to be a stressful house. We work hard to make sure it's a place of peace. I felt stuck and didn't know what to do.

A week or so after this conflict began, I was mulling the problem over when I heard the Lord tell me the same thing He'd told me on the airplane: *I want to teach your kids the power of prayer.* I told SeaJay and we gathered the kids together. I explained that we were going to pray regularly together for the cat and dog to start getting along. For the next couple of weeks, we prayed almost every night. Sometimes I had to drag them a bit (my son, Lake, usually lay there like we were torturing him), but we kept at it. They were not long prayers, but I had each of my kids pray over the situation. During one of the prayers, the Bible verse about the lion lying down with the lamb popped into my head, and I said, "I know this seems a bit cheesy, but I feel like we are to pray that the cat and dog will lie down together like the lion and the lamb." I felt a little silly praying such a significant verse over this situation, but I did it anyway.

Within two weeks of consistent prayer, things began to shift. The dog stopped growling at the cat. They started to play together. And then one day, I looked up and saw our dog lying down next to the cat at the top of the stairs. I called my kids to witness the scene. "That's what we prayed for!" Today this dog and cat are the best of buds. Every time I see them playing, God reminds me of how He used a stressful situation in our family to teach my kids the power of prayer. If the dog and cat had gotten along right away, my kids would have missed a powerful truth God wanted to teach them. When we are ungrateful, we miss what God is trying to do. When we are thankful, it shifts our perspective to understand more clearly the things God wants to accomplish.

See Abundance

My friend Zack Curry, who is on staff with us at Jesus Culture, is one of the most positive people I know. One day, Zack and I drove to the Bay Area with a couple other friends and had a great time there, but we hit some crazy traffic on the way home. Traffic is one of those things that can really wear down my patience. I hate sitting in traffic and cannot see any redeeming quality about it. Just as my frustration was starting to grow, Zack turned to the rest of us, grinning, and said, "Guys, what a great opportunity to spend more time together."

I looked at him and thought, *Are we even in the same car?* We were. Zack just had a different perspective that led him to focus on different things. My focus was on what wasn't happening—getting home quickly—while Zack's focus was on what was happening—spending time with the people in the car. It's amazing how a difference in perspective can cause two people in the same situation to have a completely different experience.

The practice of giving thanks shifts our focus from the negative to the positive like nothing else. It requires us to see the good in our lives, and even to see the good in the painful, difficult, and challenging things, rather than the negative. It requires us to look at what is happening instead of what isn't happening. Ultimately, it points our attention to what the Father is doing in our situation, rather than what He isn't doing. This leads to our staying aware of the greater reality of abundance that we're called to live in and operate from as His sons and daughters. Faith is focused on and operates from the reality of the Father's abundance, and thankfulness keeps us aware of the abundance. If we're focused on what we lack or what isn't happening, we won't operate with faith.

In John's account of Jesus' miracle of feeding the five thousand (which, again, was probably more like feeding the fifteen to twenty thousand), we see Him teaching His disciples how to shift their focus from lack to abundance, and from the circumstances to the Father, through thanksgiving. The first thing Jesus did was to expose their lack-based perspective on the crowd's need and how to meet it. "Jesus lifted up His eyes, and seeing a great multitude coming toward Him, He said to Philip, 'Where shall we buy bread, that these may eat?' But this He said to test him, for He Himself knew what He would do. Philip answered Him, 'Two hundred denarii worth of bread is not sufficient for them, that every one of them may have a little.' One of His disciples, Andrew, Simon Peter's brother, said to Him, 'There is a lad here who has five barley loaves and two small fish, but what are they among so many?'" (John 6:5–9 NKJV).

Philip essentially said, "Here's what we don't have to meet this need." He saw only what they lacked. Andrew said, "Here's what we have, but it's not enough." He allowed lack to diminish the value of what they had. Jesus, in contrast, took what they had and gave thanks. "Jesus took the loaves, and when He had given thanks He distributed them to the disciples, and the disciples to those sitting down; and likewise of the fish, as much as they wanted" (John 6:11 NKJV). Jesus gave thanks before the miracle, not after, because His gratitude gave Him eyes of faith to see the Father's power and provision. His gratitude and faith positioned Him to see the invisible reality of the Father's abundance manifest in the visible.

Thankfulness lifts our gaze from the need to the one who meets our needs, from the gifts to the Giver, from the provision to the Provider. It keeps us aware of His generous heart and character and who He has promised to be to us as our good Father. Remember, faith is not mental assent to truth but relational trust in a Person. To walk in trust, we need to stay aware of whom we're trusting. As when Peter walked on the water, our faith works when our eyes are locked on the Person who told us to come to Him (Matt. 14:28–30). Thankfulness helps us keep looking for and at Him in every situation, which positions us to receive whatever He wants to release to us.

The enemy knows that if he can get our eyes off the Father and onto anything else, he can disable our faith, so he works to distract us. His efforts to distract us are sometimes so extreme that it reminds me of the crazy fans who wave thunder sticks during an NBA basketball game. Thunder sticks are inflatable tubes that they drop from the ceiling for the seats directly behind the opposing team's basket. Whenever the opposing team is shooting a free throw, the crowd pulls them out and starts waving them to distract the shooter. Those fans go wild trying to get the players to miss their shots! But the seasoned players don't even see those fans waving thunder sticks. They are so locked in on the basket, nothing can intrude on their focus. That's how we need to be with the Father. No matter what is going on around us, we don't have to let it take our gaze from Him. Giving thanks in everything keeps our gaze where it needs to be.

When we keep our gaze on the Father, we don't get distracted by lack, and we don't diminish what we have in our hands. The disciples dismissed the five loaves and two fish because it was so little. They even despised it because it seemed so useless in light of the need in front of them. But Jesus was grateful for what He had, because He saw that the Father had provided it as a seed to be multiplied. Gratitude helps us see that everything the Father gives us is connected to His unlimited resources and helps us lean in, expecting Him to release those resources to meet our needs. This was Paul's confidence: "My God shall supply all your need according to His riches in glory by Christ Jesus" (Phil. 4:19 NKJV).

A lifestyle of thanksgiving reminds us that our Father never leaves us empty-handed. If we start to feel like He isn't really doing much in our lives or moving on our behalf, it's probably because we've gotten distracted and become negative and ungrateful. We're dismissing the seed He's put in our hands to multiply by faith in Him. If we want to see where He's at work—because He always is at work in our lives—then we need to start giving thanks again. A great place to start is by thanking Jesus for the cross. It's amazing to me how easily we can end up living without gratitude simply because we have forgotten the work of the cross in our lives. The longer I live, the more grateful I become for the price Jesus paid for me. The thought that Jesus was whipped, beaten, mocked, scorned, and nailed to a cross as a criminal and then died for me to save me from death and bring me to life in Him just wrecks me with gratitude. The cross is where we see the Father's generous heart to give us all things. "He who did not spare His own Son, but delivered Him up for us all, how shall He not with Him also freely give us all things?" (Rom. 8:32 NKJV). If you are struggling to live with gratitude, start at the cross and from there look at the rest of your life. Giving thanks for *that* in everything is a catalyst for faith.

Putting Gas in the Truck

Thankfulness is an inside job that is not connected to outside forces. Thankfulness begins when we take responsibility for this reality. To live thankful means you are not blaming other people or circumstances for your lack of joy or gratefulness.

The college I attended was a ten-hour drive from where I grew up in Northern California. I made the trip home a few times a year, usually carpooling with a couple other guys who also lived up north. One of these trips I took with my buddies Pete and Steve in Pete's truck. It was definitely close quarters with three college kids crammed in that cab. About eight and a half hours into the drive, we made our last stop to get gas. We pulled up to the gas pump, jumped out, and headed for the gas station—Pete to pay for the gas, Steve to get snacks, and me to use the restroom. After we had finished up, we got back in the truck and drove off, anxious to get home. But about fifteen minutes down the highway, the truck started to sputter and lost power. We coasted to the side of the freeway and began trying to figure out what was wrong with Pete's truck. The oil gauge was fine. The temperature gauge was fine. Then I looked at the gas gauge. It was on empty.

"Did you put gas in the truck at the gas station?" I asked Pete.

"No," he answered. "I paid for it but thought Steve was putting it in."

We both turned to look at Steve. "Did you put gas in the truck?"

"No, I was getting snacks and thought Banning was putting the gas in."

Then Pete and Steve both looked at me.

"Don't look at me, fellas. I was using the restroom and thought Pete was putting gas in."

We had driven to the gas station, paid for the gas, gotten snacks, used the restroom, and then pulled away without ever putting gas in the truck. Each of us thought someone else was going to do it.

This is how many Christians live. They think someone else is going to take care of making sure they have their hearts supplied with hope, peace, and joy. Someone else is responsible for what is happening inside them. Your internal world is not someone else's responsibility. We tend to make excuses for our attitude of ungratefulness because we think someone or something else is responsible. But we can and must be thankful no matter what our circumstances are because thankfulness is an inside job. And when we are thankful, we live from a place of abundance where faith comes alive. Faith is required on this three-mile walk, and thankfulness is the will of God for our lives.

10

The Moment for Faith

Saul and Jonathan both acted in a moment of crisis. Saul, seeing his men flee in terror as the Philistine army amassed, and growing desperate as Samuel delayed in coming to make sacrifices to the Lord, took matters into his own hands. He tried to calm the people and force God to move by making the sacrifices himself. This choice cost him the kingdom. He was not a man after God's heart because he didn't trust God. He didn't act in faith.

Jonathan saw his father and their terrified army of six hundred huddling in their camp, waiting to be descended on by "thirty thousand chariots and six thousand horsemen, and people as the sand which is on the seashore" (1 Sam. 13:5 NKJV), and he also took matters into his own hands. But he acted from faith. He came up with a plan that depended totally on God to fulfill it. He didn't try to manipulate or make demands from God; he simply positioned himself and his armor-bearer where they could see what God was doing and partner with Him. They prepared for the battle by crossing that three-mile valley, waited for His signal to engage the enemy, and then stepped boldly into the fight, confident that God had given them the victory.

Moments of crisis, moments when no human solution is obvious, are either moments when we act in fear and make things worse or moments of opportunity for faith. I don't want to miss my moments, and I don't want you to miss your moments. Individually and corporately as the body of Christ, we are facing and will face moments of opportunity to trust and partner with God and see Him move in incredible ways on our behalf. The challenge is that they will appear as opportunities for faith, and we will step into them with boldness, only if we have what Jonathan had—a heart of faith, eyes of faith, and a posture of faith.

In the previous two chapters, we looked at how we need to keep the supply lines of hope and peace flowing to our hearts and keep our eyes seeing correctly through thankfulness. Now it's time to look at how to posture ourselves to engage the moment before us with bold faith. The posture of faith is a set of habitual behaviors we must establish in our lives on the three-mile walk—the habits of meditating and remembering the testimonies of God, declaring His promises, waiting for Him with preparation and persistence, being specific in our requests of Him, and humbly using that which He purchased for us. These habits will help us to act with faith in our moment.

Bold Faith Meditates and Remembers

Psalm 77 begins with the speaker seeking God "in the day of [his] trouble" (Ps. 77:2 NKJV). We don't know what this trouble was, but we know he was in over his head, because he was asking the questions we start to ask in impossible situations: "Where is God? Where are His favor and His promises? Has He forgotten about me? Is He mad at me?" One of the reasons I love the Psalms is that they show us it's okay to wrestle with faith and be brutally honest with God about it. Many of us have this idea that God can't handle our honesty. The truth is that He *loves* our honesty. He is thrilled when we come to Him as our authentic selves and trust Him enough to show Him our questions and pain and doubts so He can help us through them.

The other reason I love the Psalms is that they give us clear pathways for how to find God and follow Him from the place of fear and doubt to the place of faith. Look at what the psalmist does next.

> I said, "This is my anguish;
> But I will remember the years of the right hand of the
>   Most High."
> I will remember the works of the LORD;
> Surely I will remember Your wonders of old.
> I will also meditate on all Your work,
> And talk of Your deeds.
>
> —PSALM 77:10–12 NKJV

For the rest of the psalm, the speaker rehearses the story of the exodus. This psalmist, Asaph, lived hundreds of years after God led His people out of Egypt, but the memory of that event had been carefully preserved and passed down through the practice of rehearsing and meditating on the testimony, which God commanded His people to do continuously (Deut. 6:6–9). Through meditating on the testimony, the psalmist remembered not only what God did in the past but who God is and will be in his present situation. Remembering shifted him into the posture of faith.

It's amazing how we so easily forget what God has done. Matthew's gospel records an occasion when the disciples forget that they had twice seen Jesus multiply bread and fish for multitudes.

Jesus had just finished dealing with a group of religious leaders who came to test Him, and warned His disciples, "Take heed and beware of the leaven of the Pharisees and the Sadducees" (Matt. 16:6 NKJV). This statement flew over the disciples' heads. For some reason, they thought Jesus was criticizing them for not bringing bread on this leg of their journey. Jesus seemed genuinely shocked by how they interpreted His words. "Jesus, being aware of it, said to them, 'O you of little faith, why do you reason among yourselves because you have brought no bread? Do you not yet understand, or remember the five loaves of the five thousand and how many baskets you took up? Nor the seven loaves of the four thousand and how many large baskets you took up? How is it you do not understand that I did not speak to you concerning bread?—but to beware of the leaven of the Pharisees and Sadducees'" (Matt. 16:8–11 NKJV).

Jesus basically said, "I'm telling you about one problem, and you think I'm talking about another problem you have already seen Me solve—and solved with Me—on two occasions. The only way you'd think I was talking about that other problem is if you didn't understand that we already solved it, or forgot that we had." Jesus expected His disciples to learn from their past experiences with Him, in a way that formed their ability to perceive and respond in their present situation.

The problem was that the disciples had never moved those miracles from their short-term memory to their long-term memory. Scientists tell us that our storage capacity for memory is virtually unlimited; they estimate that our brains can store roughly 2.5 petabytes of data, which is about three hundred years' worth of TV. However, *what* gets stored depends on what we deem important. The brain is constantly processing the flood of information it encounters every day, assigning each package of data a different level of importance and storing that data accordingly. Short-term memory, closely related to working memory, is information we hold on to before either dismissing it or transferring it to long-term memory. The most basic way our brains determine what information is important enough to store in long-term memory is repetition. Repeated experience tells our brains to pay attention and keep that information in a retrievable place, because we'll probably need it again. Repetition can be built into our experience simply by the nature of it (like many things we encounter daily) or created by our choice. This is the nature of every type of active learning, education, training, or discipline: we position ourselves to encounter the same information again and again so it moves from our short-term memory to our long-term memory.

The disciples misunderstood Jesus' warning about the Pharisees and Sadducees because the two miraculous feedings they had witnessed and participated in never really made it to their long-term memory, and that happened because they hadn't assigned them the importance they deserved in the first place. If they had, they would have taken the time to rehearse the experiences again and again, pondering and meditating on what had happened so that they could understand what they revealed about Jesus, His character, and how He wanted to show up in their relationship. This understanding would have formed their perception so that when they found themselves in a situation in which provision was needed, it would trigger their memory. "Oh, this is another situation where we need bread. The last two times that happened, Jesus multiplied it for us. Jesus, here we are again. We're going to position ourselves with faith to see You be Yourself in this situation, like You did in the past." We so easily forget what God has done in our lives when we're facing the pressure of a situation in which faith is needed.

When God shows up in power in our lives, He's not just trying to show off or solve the immediate problem. He's teaching us who He is and wants to be in our lives. Faith comes from understanding the nature and character of God. The way we show we have learned our lesson is by expecting Him to show up in the same way again.

God challenged me on this a couple of years ago, when we found ourselves facing a fresh set of financial challenges as a ministry. (Throughout this book, I've primarily used the example of finances because it's one of the challenges we can all relate to.) Feeling overwhelmed, I took the problem to the Lord in prayer. Not long after I started praying, I heard Him say, *Don't act like I'm not the God who multiplies bread and extends cash flow projections.* It had been only two years since we prayed every day as a team and watched Him miraculously extend our cash flow month after month. Yet there I was, facing the same problem as though I hadn't seen Him solve it before. I realized that even though I had experienced that year of miraculous cash flow, I hadn't learned from it the way I needed to. I had celebrated it but hadn't locked it in my long-term memory so that when the next financial miracle was needed, I would position myself with faith to see God show up in the same way.

God expects us to pay attention when He does something. He expects us to meditate on it and allow the revelation of who He is to sink deeply into our understanding. And He expects us to show up at the next situation with a long-term memory that will be triggered so we can respond in a way that shows we remember who He is.

The Hebrew word for meditate is *hagah*, which means "to moan, growl, utter, muse, mutter, meditate, devise, plot, speak."[13] There's a reason why so much learning in childhood revolves around repeatedly reciting and chanting things aloud. Using our voices and ears to reinforce information creates sensory data for our brains to store and increases the likelihood that it will be memorized—moved from short-term memory to long-term memory. If we're going to remember what God has done, we need to make it a practice to talk about it to ourselves and with others.

Writing is another great way to meditate on the testimonies of God. As I've shared, I like to make lists. My "Things God Has Already Taken Care Of" list may have things on it that are yet to be resolved, but I know they will be because I have seen Him solve the same problem in the past. I keep those lists and go back to them as a testimony of how God did take care of those things. I am using testimonies to see my future with faith.

As with the psalmist of Psalm 77 remembering the exodus, many of the testimonies I remember are not even mine; I wasn't there when they happened. But that doesn't matter. God expected future generations of Israelites to position themselves with faith in Him after hearing what He had done for their ancestors. He expects us to position ourselves with faith when we hear what He's done both in the past and in our present generation, as much as by remembering what He has done in our lives. God is no respecter of persons; what He does for one person, He will do for me. This means that I will often find the faith I need for breakthrough in my present situation in someone else's story. It also means I am accountable, when I hear other people's testimonies of what God has done in their lives, to believe that who God has been for them, He will be for me.

Bold Faith Speaks

Scripture establishes two important truths about every human being. First, our words are powerful. We were made in the image of the God who spoke the universe into existence. Second, our words flow from our hearts. "A good man out of the good treasure of his heart brings forth good; and an evil man out of the evil treasure of his heart brings forth evil. For out of the abundance of the heart his mouth speaks" (Luke 6:45 NKJV). Whatever spiritual reality our hearts are attached to by faith determines whether we use the power of our words for good or evil.

One of the most fascinating stories in Scripture about the power of our words is the story of Zacharias and Elizabeth, parents of John the Baptist. As the priest Zacharias was performing his duties in the temple, the angel Gabriel appeared to him and announced that his prayers for a son had been heard and were about to be answered. Not only would he have a son; this son would be a Nazirite filled with the Holy Spirit from birth who would minister in the spirit of Elijah, turn the hearts of the people back to God, and prepare the way for the Lord's coming. In response to this incredible announcement, Zacharias said, "How shall I know this? For I am an old man, and my wife is well advanced in years" (Luke 1:18 NKJV). Instead of faith, the words that came from his mouth revealed a heart full of fear. So Gabriel said, "Behold, you will be mute and not able to speak until the day these things take place, because you did not believe my words which will be fulfilled in their own time" (Luke 1:20 NKJV).

God put Zacharias on mute because his words were full of unbelief. Many of us read that and think God was punishing Zacharias, but God was trying to help Zacharias. He was saying, "Zacharias, I need you to understand that if you keep talking, you could undermine or disqualify yourself from the plans and purpose I'm trying to accomplish through you and your family. I'm going to give you some time to work on your heart so you can start releasing faith into this situation." One of the best things you can do if there is unbelief in your heart is stop talking. Allow faith to grow in your heart so that it will come out of your mouth. Beautifully, that's exactly what Zacharias did. When John was born, Zacharias released words of faith on a writing tablet: "His name is John" (Luke 1:63). Immediately he found his voice fully restored.

I'm not sure we truly understand the power and weight of our words, because we can be so careless with what we say. Our Father wants us to appreciate and understand the responsibility that comes with having powerful words. As a father, I can relate to this desire when it comes to entrusting my kids with anything powerful—for example, a car. When my eldest daughter, Ellianna, was working toward her driver's license, it became clear that SeaJay and I had done a great job of instilling confidence in her ability to tackle challenges like learning to drive. She took her driver's license test and got a perfect score on her exam. I was proud of her, but I remember one moment when we were in the car and I was trying to teach her something and she disagreed with me.

"Elli, I've been driving for more than twenty years," I said. "You've been driving for three months."

Unimpressed, she looked at me and said, "Dad, I've been driving for four months."

While I was amused that she believed that an extra month was the difference maker, in that moment, I wondered whether we had done a good enough job of balancing our daughter's confidence with a healthy dose of reality. I didn't want anything to dim her confidence or make her scared of driving, but I did want her to understand the immense responsibility of getting behind the wheel of a vehicle, and what it could cost her if she wasn't careful with the power she possessed while driving.

We need to understand that our words are powerful and be careful to use that power well. When we speak words of faith, we partner with the plans and purposes of God. When we speak words of unbelief, we resist His plans and purposes. Unbelief is not a lack of belief; it is belief in the wrong thing. It is trusting the lies of the enemy rather than God's truth. It is being more connected to your circumstances than to what God has said. Zacharias was more connected to the circumstances and his and his wife's ages than to what God had said, and that's what came out of his mouth. In His mercy, God kept Zacharias from using the power of his words in a destructive way.

One of the reasons why God commands us to meditate on His Word and His testimonies is that the more we speak His words, the more we hide them in our hearts. The more His Word is hidden in our hearts, the more it comes out of our mouths. Psalm 119:11 says, "Your word I have hidden in my heart, that I might not sin against You" (NKJV). We need to cram so much Word into our hearts that what comes out of our mouths is faith. When I think of having the Word crammed into my heart, I think of riding the subway in New York City. I once rode the subway on a weekday afternoon, and it was packed with people. When I pointed this out to the man who was with me, he said, "Oh, this is nothing. Every morning, I get on at 7:00 a.m. and have to turn backward and shove my way in; I can barely squeeze in for the doors to shut." I didn't think it was possible to get more people on that train, but apparently it was. That's the picture we need to have when we think about hiding the Word of God in our hearts—that when we pull up to the train station and unbelief and lies are trying to get in, there just isn't any room to fit because our hearts are too full of His Word. Instead, when the doors open, what spills out are His promises and His testimonies.

I recently met with a senior pastor who had just planted a church. When our conversation turned to the subject of finances, I began to tell him testimonies of God's provision on our journey of planting Jesus Culture Sacramento. I told him one story about an older woman, an intercessor, who loved our team dearly and prayed for us faithfully over the years as our ministry grew. She often came to our staff meetings to pray over our team. Sadly, shortly after we moved to Sacramento to start our church, she became sick and passed away. Our hearts were sad when we heard of this loss. A year after she died, another member of that intercessors group asked to meet with me. When I sat down with her, she told me that our faithful intercessor had called her attorney a week before her death and instructed him to put Jesus Culture in her will. The other member then reached across the table and handed me a check for a significant amount of money. No one even knew this woman had money. I couldn't believe it. The money couldn't have come at a more perfect time in our journey as a church. I was moved and awestruck that God had stirred the heart of this beautiful woman to change her will, because He knew we would need the money a year later. After years of loving this bunch of young leaders who dreamed of changing a generation, she was still investing in us even from heaven.

I also shared the story of a pastor in Texas who heard me on a podcast talking about our journey of raising money for a building. He and his church were also believing God for a building, and he knew right away that their church was to take an offering for our building as if it were their own. He announced to the church that in a month they were going to take an offering for us and instructed them to give as if it were their building. They weren't a very large group, but they took an offering and sent us a generous check. I was floored that a church and a pastor I had never met would do that for us. I have the letter that came with the check framed on my office wall to remind me of the faithfulness of God as we continue to move forward and believe Him for the provision needed to fulfill the vision He has given us. I later learned that when it came time for the church in Texas to start raising money for their building, they took an offering that was ten times the amount they sent to us. As I shared these testimonies with the pastor in my office, you could feel the faith rise in our hearts. God is the God who stirs the heart of the intercessor and moves a church in Texas to provide for us in our moment of need.

When we declare the testimonies and promises of God in faith over a situation, we release power for God to come and do it again. Great boldness comes when we say what God has said and done, and is saying and doing, because we are confident that He will back up His word and do it again. This is the boldness of faith! If you look at where *boldness* shows up in the New Testament, it typically has to do with boldness of speech.

> When they saw the boldness of Peter and John, and perceived that they were uneducated and untrained men, they marveled. And they realized that they had been with Jesus.
>
> —ACTS 4:13 NKJV

> "Lord, look on their threats, and grant to Your servants that with all boldness they may speak Your word, by stretching out Your hand to heal, and that signs and wonders may be done through the name of Your holy Servant Jesus."
>
> And when they had prayed, the place where they were assembled together was shaken; and they were all filled with the Holy Spirit, and they spoke the word of God with boldness.
>
> —ACTS 4:29–31 NKJV

> Since we have such hope, we use great boldness of speech.
>
> —2 CORINTHIANS 3:12 NKJV

Great is my boldness of speech toward you, great is my boasting on your behalf. I am filled with comfort. I am exceedingly joyful in all our tribulation.

—2 CORINTHIANS 7:4 NKJV

The Greek word for boldness, *parresia*, means "freedom in speaking, unreservedness in speech, free and fearless confidence, cheerful courage, boldness, confidence."[14] If you look at the great heroes of faith in the Bible, they all had moments when they spoke up and declared God's word over the situation. Their boldness to speak released God's plans and purposes into their circumstances, changing not only their futures but history itself.

Bold Faith Waits

The story of Bartimaeus is a powerful picture of bold faith that speaks up. Bartimaeus was blind, which at that time and place in history relegated him to being a lifelong beggar. He could not contribute to society in any way. The only way he could provide for himself or his family was to rely on others to take him to the outskirts of town every day to sit and beg for alms. However, while Bartimaeus was financially poor, he was rich in the currency of heaven—faith.

Then it happened, as He was coming near Jericho, that a certain blind man sat by the road begging. And hearing a multitude passing by, he asked what it meant. So they told him that Jesus of Nazareth was passing by. And he cried out, saying, "Jesus, Son of David, have mercy on me!"

Then those who went before warned him that he should be quiet; but he cried out all the more, "Son of David, have mercy on me!"

So Jesus stood still and commanded him to be brought to Him. And when he had come near, He asked him, saying, "What do you want Me to do for you?"

He said, "Lord, that I may receive my sight."

Then Jesus said to him, "Receive your sight; your faith has made you well." And immediately he received his sight, and followed Him, glorifying God. And all the people, when they saw it, gave praise to God.

—LUKE 18:35–43 NKJV

Think about how profound this statement is: "Jesus stood still." Jesus, the creator of the universe, the one who spoke the world into existence and holds the stars in His hands, stopped for this poor beggar. Almost no one, except for those who felt pity, stopped for Bartimaeus. But Bartimaeus got Jesus' attention, not through the volume of his voice or the commotion of the people trying to quiet him but through his faith.

There's really only one explanation for why Bartimaeus responded the way he did when someone told him that Jesus was passing by. Bartimaeus had been waiting for Jesus. We don't know how old he was or how long he had sat begging, but at some point news had reached him about a man traveling the countryside who healed the blind, and Bartimaeus believed that this man could heal him. He believed He was the Son of David, the Messiah, come to rescue Israel. He put his faith in Him before he ever met Him. Perhaps he prayed that God would lead this Son of David past the place where he sat each day on the roadside. All we know is that he was waiting with a level of anticipation that led him to boldly raise his voice the minute he heard Jesus was nearby.

Waiting in faith is very different from passing time. Life is full of waiting periods, and most of us take a passive posture when we're waiting; these days, we spend it distracting ourselves on our phones. Waiting in faith is completely different. One of the Hebrew words for wait is *qavah*, which means "to wait, look for, hope, expect . . . to wait or look eagerly for . . . to lie in wait for . . . to wait for, linger for."[15] It's a posture of actively leaning forward in anticipation for something to come. It's the kind of waiting I did the day my dad brought home my first car when I was sixteen. He had to drive out of town to get the car, and I spent the whole day in eager anticipation for him to return. I did nothing but wait for that car to pull up in our driveway. I got up constantly and looked out the window, then walked out to the driveway and looked down the street for any sign of my dad's arrival. That's what it looks like to wait in faith—to eagerly look for signs of our Father and what He has promised.

Isaiah 64:4 says, "Since the beginning of the world men have not heard nor perceived by the ear, nor has the eye seen any God besides You, who acts for the one who waits for Him" (NKJV). The word translated "waits" here is *chakah*, which means to wait, to tarry, to wait in ambush, or long for.[16] The idea of waiting in ambush is the picture of a hunter waiting for his prey. Hunters don't just wander out into the wilderness hoping to stumble across a deer. They study the ways and paths of deer so they can lie in wait for them to come. They know that deer travel by certain routes—along the borders of forests or fields or through natural funnels of vegetation. They know that deer revisit the places where they scrape their antlers. They know where and when they eat and how they respond to different topographies and weather. All of this knowledge helps hunters discover the best place to set up an ambush.

This is the picture David uses in Psalm 25:4 when he says, "Show me your ways, LORD, teach me your paths." He's saying, "God, I want to know how You move. I want to be able to anticipate where You're going to be so I can position myself where You'll be." This is why having a firm biblical foundation is critical to our faith. If we are going to set our lives up in anticipation for Him to move, we need to know His character, how He works, where and when He shows up, and what He responds to. Studying the Scriptures and testimonies of God teaches us His paths and His ways. Scripture also teaches us that waiting in faith, leaning in and setting an ambush for God to move, requires preparation and persistence.

When we believe someone, we prepare. If I invite someone over for dinner on Thursday at 7:00 p.m. and they tell me they will come over, then I begin to get ready for them. I go to the store and buy food. I clean the house. On Wednesday, I might start prepping the food. On Thursday, I start cooking it. I set the table and buy some fresh flowers to decorate it. If someone asks me why I'm shopping and cooking and getting the house ready, I say that my friend is coming over. My actions show that I believed them when they said they would come. If I didn't believe them, then I wouldn't prepare.

You can tell whether someone believes God by looking at what they are preparing for. Hebrews 11:7 says that by faith Noah prepared an ark. By faith the widow gathered vessels to prepare for the miraculous provision of oil Elisha had promised her (2 Kings 4:1–7). When God speaks a word to us, there will be preparation involved. It's one of the ways we prove that we believe what He said. Conversely, when we don't prepare, it shows that we don't believe God. We know Peter didn't really believe Jesus when He told him to cast his nets out again, because Peter cast only one net. He wasn't prepared for the miraculous haul of fish that came in, and because of that, the net began to break (Luke 5:4–8). Our lives should consist of building arks, gathering vessels, and casting nets in preparation for what God is going to do.

Bold faith, faith that waits, is also persistent. Again, faith means believing that God is "a rewarder of those who *diligently* seek Him" (Heb. 11:6 NKJV, emphasis added). Diligence is careful or persistent work or effort. One of the reasons why Jesus told us to seek God as a child is not because children have simple faith but because this faith manifests in persistence. Children are the most persistent people on the planet. If you're a parent, you know this well. You can tell them no, and five minutes later you're saying yes, just because of their persistence. This is the picture Jesus paints in his parables of the persistent neighbor (Luke 11:5–8) and the persistent widow (Luke 18:1–8). The Father loves our persistence, not because He wants us to think we have to twist His arm to convince Him to do what He said He'll do but because it shows Him that we believe Him. We understand His character and nature as a Father. This is why Jesus urged us, "Ask and you'll receive. Seek and you'll discover. Knock on heaven's door, and it will one day open for you. Every persistent person will get what he asks for. Every persistent seeker will discover what he needs. And everyone who knocks persistently will one day find an open door" (Luke 11:9–10 TPT).

Bold Faith Is Specific

When Jesus came to Bartimaeus and asked, "What can I do for you?" Bartimaeus didn't give some general answer. He said clearly what he wanted: "Lord, that I may receive my sight" (Luke 18:41 NKJV). Bold faith is specific faith. It is not a vague belief in something; it is a clear expectation we have of the Lord.

I once heard Kris Vallotton tell the story of how his house was paid off by a man who approached him at a meeting. It's a powerful story of God's abundant, radical generosity and provision for us, but the thing that challenged and convicted me most about the story was how it began. Kris was lying in bed one night with his wife, Kathy, talking about his heart to minister to leaders around the world and how he knew they needed to lower their expenses in order for him to do that. They stopped in the middle of the conversation, and Kris prayed a simple prayer that God would pay off their house. And then it happened! I wasn't just inspired that somebody had paid off Kris's house; I was challenged and convicted by Kris and Kathy's faith to pray for something so specific. Kris didn't think twice about coming to God with a specific prayer request of that magnitude. I realized I tended to be much more general when I asked God for things. Sometimes that's simply because I don't know what to ask for, but other times I know I'm being vague because I don't want to risk disappointment. I'm scared to believe God for something specific.

You may have heard that the best way to achieve goals is to make sure they are SMART—specific, measurable, actionable, relevant, and time-bound. "Specific" is the first criteria for setting goals we will achieve. We shouldn't just say we want to get healthy this year; we should be specific about the number of times we want to go to the gym every week. The reason many of us never set these types of goals for ourselves is that the minute we get specific with our goals, we set ourselves up for the possibility of failure. To avoid failure, we stay general in our goals. But without specific goals, we never end up achieving much of anything. In the same way, many of us try to avoid disappointment by staying general in our prayers; that way, we can avoid the possibility of God not answering those specific prayers. But without specific prayers of faith, we never get to see specific answers that grow our faith. You may have a financial need in your life, such as to pay off debt or meet expenses. Figure out the exact amount you need and then pray for that amount. Get specific with your prayer.

SeaJay and I married at twenty-one and became pregnant with our first child five months later. We were so excited about becoming parents. Shortly after we found out SeaJay was pregnant, someone recommended a book called *Supernatural Childbirth* by Jackie Mize. In the book, Mize shares testimonies from her pregnancies and teaching from Scripture encouraging women to approach their pregnancies and delivery from faith rather than fear. We both read the book and were immediately impacted and challenged by it. As a man, I don't talk about pregnancy and childbirth often, but for so many people, this subject and experience has been surrounded by fear. After reading this book, SeaJay and I felt challenged to believe God for something different from the stories and advice we were hearing from so many people. We began to pray for specific things, and one of those things was that SeaJay would have a four-hour delivery. When we shared this with people, most of them looked at us like we were just young, naive people with no clue about what SeaJay was about to experience. But when Ellianna was born, the delivery took exactly four hours. We got to the hospital at 6:30 a.m., and she was born at 10:30 a.m. Every other specific prayer request we had made about the delivery was answered as well. So when SeaJay became pregnant with Raya, we got even more specific with our prayers. There were things we didn't even know to pray about for the first birth. This time we prayed for an afternoon delivery so SeaJay wouldn't be as exhausted as she was with her first birth, which had been so early in the morning. Sure enough, Raya was born in the afternoon.

I would never want to suggest that if someone has had a difficult pregnancy, it is because of their lack of faith. I am very aware that sometimes we pray specific prayers and things don't always turn out exactly the way we ask. However, we need to be specific if we want to pray with bold faith. Yes, it may mean risking disappointment or having people see us as naive. But getting specific shows God that we are willing to risk these things to see Him show up on our behalf. It shows that we understand He wants us to come to Him like Bartimaeus and ask Him for exactly what we want Him to do for us.

Bold Faith Is Humble

One of the things I love about Bartimaeus is that when everyone else told him to shrink back, he "cried out all the more" (Luke 18:39 NKJV). Bartimaeus was not being defiant, arrogant, or belligerent. He was being quite humble. He was doing what we are commanded to do in Hebrews: "Let us therefore come boldly to the throne of grace, that we may obtain mercy and find grace to help in time of need" (Heb. 4:16 NKJV). Grace is something that God gives only to the humble. "God resists the proud, but gives grace to the humble" (James 4:6 NKJV).

Many times, we don't step out into boldness because it feels arrogant. True boldness isn't arrogant; it is courageous. And genuine courage is born only of humility. Humility is being grateful for the gift that was given to you, and the best expression of gratitude is using that gift. Being bold in our faith is simply a matter of using what God has given to us—access to Him and His kingdom.

I love it when people use something I bought for them. It is a bit of a joke in my family that I don't mind spending money on a gift, but I hate spending money if it's not the right gift and the person won't use it. When it is the right gift and they do use it, it makes me so happy. I will talk about that gift for months afterward, the little gifts as well as the big. I bought my wife a kitchen cart that is a cutting board, and it makes me so happy every time I see her cutting things on it. I love seeing our cat playing on the cat structure I bought for her. My wife and kids send me pictures whenever they're using whatever I bought them, because they know how much I love to see them using my gifts. Never in a million years would I see them using my gifts as arrogant. I see it as love.

Now imagine that someone worked hard for ten years, saved the money to buy me a nice car because they knew I needed it, and called me to tell me the car was sitting at their house waiting for me to pick it up. If I never went and picked it up, what would that mean? It would mean either that I didn't trust the person to give me a car with no strings attached or that I was too proud to receive something like that for free. It's arrogant and mistrustful *not* to receive a gift from someone, and humble and trusting to receive it.

Or what if I did pick it up, expressed my gratitude for their gift, but then never drove the car? It would bring no joy to the person who sacrificed to purchase that car for me if it just sat in my driveway, gathering dust. But imagine the joy it would bring that person when they saw me drive by in the car they sacrificed for. It would make their sacrifice worth it. The best way I can show them gratitude is not only to pick up the car but to use it.

Jesus said, "Do not fear, little flock, for it is your Father's good pleasure to give you the kingdom" (Luke 12:32 NKJV). There is so much more of the kingdom available to us that we don't access. It's humble to take God at His word and access it. It's not humble to let it sit there untouched and unused.

Of course, another possibility is that I don't pick the car up because I have decided I can live without a car. I am going to settle for living a life limited by how far I can walk around my neighborhood or by what others are willing to bring me. I don't want the full freedom, power, and responsibility a car will bring.

Years ago, when flat-screen TVs were just coming in, SeaJay and I remodeled the downstairs of our house and bought one, along with a surround sound system. Because it was a big purchase, I made sure we had it installed properly so we could get the best experience. I was so excited to watch movies with Dolby Digital sound coming at me from all angles. But because SeaJay and I are opposites in so many areas, she wasn't as excited as I was. She was content to watch movies without the fancy surround sound, instead using the small TV speaker. She thought it was too much effort to use two remotes to turn the sound system on and then the TV. I just couldn't fathom why she would do this! Why would she not want to experience the fullness of what was available?

I realize that it doesn't really matter whether SeaJay uses the sound system we paid for, but it does matter whether we access what Jesus paid for. He laid down His life to make the full resources of the Father's kingdom available to us, and we mustn't settle for anything less. Bold faith gratefully and humbly receives this immense gift and expresses that gratitude and humility by using the Father's resources, because bold faith recognizes that this gift has come from the Father in order for us to fulfill what He has called us to be and to do in this moment.

Now Is Your Moment

"It happened one day that Jonathan the son of Saul said to the young man who bore his armor, 'Come, let us go over to the Philistines' garrison that is on the other side'" (1 Sam. 14:1 NKJV). *One day.* The tide of the battle for a nation turned in one day because one man decided to set out on a three-mile walk to engage his call. What could happen in a day because you decide to engage your call?

I challenge you: let that day be today. Set yourself fully apart for God and His purposes. Receive His courage to take the journey with Him. And commit to becoming the person of bold faith who will trust and partner with Him in every situation. Take the three-mile walk with Him, and don't miss a moment of being and doing what you were created and called to be and do.

Notes

1. "Lexicon: Strong's H3820–*leb*," *Blue Letter Bible, www.blue letterbible.org//lang/lexicon/lexicon.cfm?Strongs=H3820&t=NIV* (August 23, 2019).

2. Eric Metaxas, *Bonhoeffer: Pastor, Martyr, Prophet, Spy* (Nashville: Nelson, 2010), 82.

3. Charles H. Spurgeon, *The Complete Works of C. H. Spurgeon: Letters to My Students*, vol. 1 (Fort Collins, CO: Delmarva Publications, 2013), 73.

4. Wayne Grudem, *Systematic Theology* (Grand Rapids: Zondervan, 1994), 71.

5. C. S. Lewis, *Letters to an American Lady* (Grand Rapids: Eerdmans, 1971), 19.

6. Steve Backlund, *Let's Just Laugh at That* (Redding, CA: Steve Backlund, 2011), 7.

7. "Battlefield Medicine," *Wikipedia, https://en.wikipedia.org/wiki /Battlefield_medicine* (November 25, 2019).

8. Ibid.

9. David Bohrer, *America's Special Forces* (St. Paul, MN: MBI, 2002), 11.

10. "Lexicon: Strong's G5281–*hypomonē*," *Blue Letter Bible, www.blue letterbible.org//lang/lexicon/lexicon.cfm?Strongs=G5281&t=NKJV* (September 22, 2019).

11. Donald Grey Barnhouse, *Romans: God's Glory*, p. 18, quoted in "Lexicon: Strong's G1384–*dokimos*," *Blue Letter Bible, www.blue letterbible.org/lang/lexicon/lexicon.cfm?strongs=G1384&t=NKJV.*

12. Nowhere in Scripture do I see God using sickness as a trial in our lives. There wasn't a single person Jesus turned away, saying, "God is using this sickness to teach you something." I don't know why everyone is not healed, but I do know that it is God's will to heal you.

13. "Lexicon: Strong's H1897–*hagah*," *Blue Letter Bible, www.blue letterbible.org//lang/lexicon/lexicon.cfm?Strongs=H1897&t=NKJV* (September 29, 2019).

14. "Lexicon: Strong's G3954–*parrēsia*," *Blue Letter Bible, www.blue letterbible.org//lang/lexicon/lexicon.cfm?Strongs=G3954&t=NKJV* (September 29, 2019).

15. "Lexicon: Strong's H6960–*qavah*," *Blue Letter Bible, www.blue letterbible.org//lang/lexicon/lexicon.cfm?Strongs=H6960&t=NKJV* (September 29, 2019).

16. "Lexicon: Strong's H2442–*chakah*," *Blue Letter Bible, www.blue letterbible.org//lang/lexicon/lexicon.cfm?Strongs=H2442&t=NKJV* (September 29, 2019).

New Video Study for Your Church or Small Group

If you've enjoyed this book, now you can go deeper with the companion video Bible study!

In this five-session study, Banning Liebscher helps you apply the principles in *The Three-Mile Walk* to your life. The study guide includes video notes, group discussion questions, and personal study and reflection materials for in-between sessions.

Study Guide
9780310120551

DVD
9780310120575

Available now at your favorite bookstore,
or streaming video on StudyGateway.com.